Ree's Best
Family
Meals

Pasta & Grains

"A good pasta dinner is like a bowl of pure joy."

Poultry

49 Lime Chicken Quesadillas

50 Roast Jerk Chicken

53 Chicken–Snow Pea Stir-Fry

54 Sheet-Pan Curried Chicken

57 Turkey Burger Soup

58 Slow-Cooker White Chicken Chili

61 Instant Pot Chicken Cacciatore

62 Greek Chicken Kebabs

65 Loaded Chicken and Tater Tots

66 Greek-Style Turkey Burgers

69 Instant Pot BBQ Chicken Grain Bowls

70 Pretzel-Crusted Chicken with Broccoli

73 Grilled Chicken Salad with Blue Cheese and Berries

74 Nashville Hot Chicken Plate

77 Sheet-Pan Teriyaki Chicken

78 Chicken Caesar Milanese

*"Hooray for chicken!
It makes the
whole family happy."*

Pork

82

Grilled Pork Tenderloin
with Broccolini

85

Pork Milanese

86

Slow-Cooker Teriyaki Ribs

89

Tuscan Pork
Sheet-Pan Supper

90

Sausage and
Rice Stuffed Peppers

93

Sesame Pork Noodle Salad

94

White Pizza with Butternut
Squash and Prosciutto

97

Italian Pork Sandwiches

98

BLT Baked Potatoes

101

Pork Bánh Mì Lettuce Wraps

102

Sheet-Pan Ranch Pork
and Veggies

105

Sheet-Pan Gnocchi with
Spicy Sausage and Peppers

106

Breakfast-for-Dinner
Sandwiches

109

Rice Noodle Bowls with
Soy-Sesame Pork

110

Polenta with Sausage
and Peppers

*"Can we just talk about
how versatile pork is?!"*

Beef

114 Hawaiian Pizza Burgers

117 Hoisin Steak and Pepper Stir-Fry

118 Spicy Steak with Pimiento Cheese Grits

121 Everything Burgers

122 Steakhouse Kebabs

125 Slow-Cooker Drip Beef Sandwiches

126 Steak Sandwiches with Wasabi Cream Sauce

129 Grilled Steak Wraps with Peanut Sauce

130 Instant Pot BBQ Beef Sandwiches

133 Beef and Broccoli Stir-Fry

134 Beef Curry with Sweet Potato Noodles

137 Chili-Stuffed Zucchini Boats

138 Instant Pot Pot Roast

141 Ginger Meatballs with Sesame Broccoli

142 Peppercorn-Crusted Steak with Creamed Spinach

145 Kale Caesar Salad with Steak

146 Instant Pot Ancho Beef Chili with Sweet Potatoes

"My very first blog post was about steak—it's a big part of my life!"

Fish & Seafood

150

Sheet-Pan Salmon Puttanesca

153

Ginger Shrimp Salad

154

Coconut Curry Shrimp with Potatoes and Kale

157

Spicy Shrimp Stir-Fry with Zucchini Noodles

158

Blackened Salmon with Edamame Succotash

161

Chipotle Caesar Salad with Grilled Salmon

162

Parmesan Fish Sticks with Glazed Carrots

165

Blackened Salmon Burgers with Avocado-Lime Mayo

166

Grilled Shrimp Flatbreads

169

Sweet Chili Shrimp Sauté

"We're big on shrimp and salmon in our house— they make for quick and easy dinners!"

Our Family's Favorite Recipes

_____

_____

_____

_____

_____

_____

_____

_____

_____

_____

Pasta & Grains

"Open the foil packet at the table, then fill up your bowl!"

Foil-Packet Shrimp Pasta

Prep time: 20 min ★ Total time: 50 min ★ Serves: 4 to 6

Salt, to taste
1 pound linguine or fettuccine
3 tablespoons salted butter
3 tablespoons olive oil
1½ pounds large shrimp, peeled,
     deveined, rinsed and patted dry
4 garlic cloves, minced

½ cup dry white wine
3 14.5-ounce cans diced tomatoes
Black pepper, to taste
¼ teaspoon red pepper flakes
½ cup heavy cream, warmed
Basil and parsley leaves, torn
⅓ cup grated parmesan cheese

1. Bring a large pot of salted water to a boil. Add the pasta and cook about 2 minutes less than the time for al dente on the package. Drain.
2. Meanwhile, preheat the oven to 350˚. Heat 1 tablespoon each butter and olive oil in a large skillet over medium-high heat. Add half the shrimp, season with salt and cook until they're nicely browned and opaque, 1½ to 2 minutes, turning once. Remove them to a plate and set aside. Repeat with more butter and oil, the remaining shrimp and some salt.
3. Reduce the heat to medium. Add the remaining 1 tablespoon each butter and olive oil to the skillet. Throw in the garlic and stir to prevent it from burning, then stir in the wine. Let the liquid reduce for a couple of a minutes. Stir the tomatoes with their juices, ¾ teaspoon salt, black pepper to taste and the red pepper flakes into the sauce. Simmer for about 7 minutes.
4. Grab 2 large sheets of heavy-duty foil and overlap them by about 8 inches on a rimmed baking sheet. Pour the drained pasta onto the foil. Spoon the tomato sauce and sautéed shrimp on top, making sure you include all the juices.
5. Tightly wrap the foil into a packet, rolling up the sides so it won't leak. Bake for 15 minutes.
6. Open the foil packet right before serving, drizzle with the warm heavy cream and sprinkle with the basil, parsley and cheese. Be sure to get some of the sauce with each serving. It's heavenly!

STEP BY STEP

Rigatoni with Pesto Cream Sauce

Prep time: 20 min ★ Total time: 20 min ★ Serves: 4 to 6

Salt, to taste
1 pound mezzi rigatoni or penne
¾ cup fresh basil leaves
¾ cup grated parmesan cheese
3 tablespoons pine nuts
2 garlic cloves

Black pepper, to taste
⅓ cup extra-virgin olive oil, plus a little more if needed
3 cups cherry tomatoes
½ cup heavy cream
2 tablespoons salted butter
4 ounces goat cheese, crumbled

1 Bring a large pot of salted water to a boil. Add the pasta and cook according to the package directions.
2 Meanwhile, make the pesto: Add the basil to a food processor or blender. Add ½ cup of the parmesan, the pine nuts, garlic, and salt and pepper to taste. Turn on the machine and slowly drizzle in the olive oil. Puree until bright green and all mixed together.
3 Halve the cherry tomatoes and toss them in a bowl with ½ teaspoon salt. Set aside.
4 Heat the heavy cream in a saucepan and drop in the butter. Then pour the pesto right in.

5 Stir this together and simmer it slowly for a few minutes. At the end, dump in the remaining ¼ cup parmesan and half of the goat cheese and stir it together.
6 Drain the pasta and put it in a large serving bowl. Pour on the pesto cream, then throw in the tomatoes and any juices. Toss it all together. The hot pasta and sauce will heat the tomatoes just perfectly. Top with the remaining goat cheese and serve it right away.

STEP BY STEP

"You can get this one done in 20 minutes!"

"*It's a dreamy twist on mac and cheese!*"

Tex-Mex Mac and Cheese

Prep time: 35 min ★ Total time: 40 min ★ Serves: 4 to 6

¾ teaspoon kosher salt, plus more for the pasta
1 pound penne
1 large red onion, cut into 8 wedges
1 tablespoon olive oil
1 large poblano chile pepper,
   halved lengthwise and seeded
2 cups whole milk
1 tablespoon salted butter

2 cups shredded pepper jack cheese
   (about 8 ounces)
8 ounces processed cheese (Velveeta),
   cut into cubes
1 tablespoon chili powder
1 teaspoon ground cumin
Black pepper, to taste
1 cup frozen fire-roasted corn, thawed

1 Bring a large pot of salted water to a boil. Add the pasta and cook as the label directs. Drain.

2 Meanwhile, preheat the broiler. Toss the onion wedges with the olive oil on a baking sheet. Add the poblano cut-side down. Broil until the onion is tender and the skin on the poblano blisters, about 6 minutes. Let cool slightly.

3 Pull off the poblano skin. Roughly chop the poblano and onion. Sprinkle with ¼ teaspoon salt and set aside.

4 Heat the milk and butter in a large saucepan over medium heat until hot. Add the cheeses and stir them around a bit.

5 When the cheeses start to melt, stir in the chili powder, cumin, ½ teaspoon salt and a pinch of pepper. Keep stirring until smooth. Pour in the pasta.

6 Add the corn and charred red onion and poblano and stir until it's all combined. Let it sit over the heat for 2 minutes, stirring occasionally, to help thicken the sauce. Divide among individual bowls.

STEP BY STEP

Ravioli Primavera

Prep time: 25 min ★ Total time: 25 min ★ Serves: 4 to 6

Kosher salt, to taste

2	9-ounce packages cheese or spinach ravioli
2	tablespoons salted butter
1	onion, finely diced
3	garlic cloves, minced
1	cup broccoli florets
8	ounces thin asparagus, trimmed and cut into 1-inch pieces
¼	cup white wine
⅔	cup low-sodium chicken broth
½	cup heavy cream
1	cup frozen peas, thawed
¾	cup diced ham
½	cup prepared pesto
¼	cup grated parmesan cheese, plus more for serving

Black pepper, to taste

1. Bring a large pot of salted water to a boil. Add the ravioli and cook as the label directs.
2. Meanwhile, melt the butter in a large skillet over medium-high heat. Add the onion and garlic and cook, stirring, about 1 minute. Stir in the broccoli and cook 1 minute. Stir in the asparagus and cook 1 minute. Season with salt.
3. Splash in the wine, then the chicken broth. Cook until the liquid reduces a bit, about 3 minutes. Stir in the heavy cream and simmer 1 minute.
4. Stir in the peas and let them heat up in the sauce.
5. Stir in the ham, pesto and parmesan and let them heat a bit. Season with salt and pepper.
6. Drain the ravioli, add to the skillet and toss. Serve with more parmesan.

STEP BY STEP

"I love any kind of pasta primavera. You can make this one with tortellini, too."

"I can't be stopped with Cajun seasoning. I even put it in mashed potatoes!"

Cajun Pasta with Veggies

Prep time: 40 min ★ Total time: 40 min ★ Serves: 4 to 6

Kosher salt, to taste
1   pound fettuccine
3   tablespoons olive oil
3   tablespoons salted butter
2   large bell peppers (red and green)
3   garlic cloves, minced
4½ teaspoons Cajun seasoning,
    plus more to taste

4   Roma tomatoes, diced
1   pound white mushrooms,
    halved (or quartered if large)
2   cups low-sodium vegetable broth
½   cup white wine
1   cup heavy cream
Black pepper, to taste
8   scallions, chopped

1 Bring a pot of salted water to a boil. Add the pasta and cook as the package directs for al dente. Drain the pasta.

2 Meanwhile, heat 1 tablespoon each olive oil and butter in a large cast-iron skillet over high heat. Add the bell peppers and sprinkle with the garlic and 1½ teaspoons Cajun seasoning. Let the peppers sit a few seconds so they start to blacken on the bottom, then cook, stirring gently, about 1 minute.

3 Add the tomatoes and another 1 heaping teaspoon Cajun seasoning and cook for 30 seconds. Remove the vegetable mixture to a plate.

4 Reduce the heat to medium high. Add the remaining 2 tablespoons each olive oil and butter to the skillet, then add the mushrooms and toss. Add another 1½ teaspoons Cajun seasoning and cook, stirring, until the mushrooms start to soften, about 2 minutes.

5 Pour in the broth and wine and bring to a boil. Cook for 5 minutes, scraping the bottom of the pan. Reduce the heat to medium low, pour in the heavy cream and cook, stirring constantly, until thickened, 3 minutes. Taste and add the remaining ½ teaspoon (or more) Cajun seasoning, some black pepper and salt to taste. The sauce should be spicy!

6 Add the bell peppers and tomatoes to the sauce, including the juices from the plate. Stir and cook until bubbly, 1 to 2 minutes. Add the pasta, more salt and the scallions and toss.

STEP BY STEP

Rigatoni with Summer Vegetables

Prep time: 25 min ★ Total time: 25 min ★ Serves: 4 to 6

Kosher salt
1 pound rigatoni
2 tablespoons salted butter
2 tablespoons olive oil
2 small yellow summer squash, halved lengthwise
  and thinly sliced
4 garlic cloves, finely chopped
3 ears corn, kernels cut off
Grated zest and juice of 1 lemon
8 ounces sugar snap peas, trimmed and
  halved crosswise
Black pepper, to taste
8 ounces bocconcini (mini mozzarella balls), halved
  or quartered
½ cup grated parmesan cheese, plus more
  for topping
¼ cup chopped fresh dill

1 Bring a large pot of salted water to boil. Add the pasta and cook as the label directs for al dente.

2 Meanwhile, melt the butter with the olive oil in a large skillet over medium heat. Add the squash and toss to coat. Cook, stirring, until the squash is almost tender, about 3 minutes.

3 Add the garlic and corn kernels to the skillet and cook, tossing, until the corn is tender, 2 to 3 minutes. Ladle in ¾ cup of the pasta cooking water from the pot and add the lemon zest and juice. Bring to a boil and simmer until the liquid is reduced, 2 to 3 minutes.

4 When the pasta is about 2 minutes from being done, add the sugar snap peas to the boiling water and cook until just tender. Drain the pasta and peas together.

5 Add the pasta and peas to the skillet with the squash and corn. Add 1 teaspoon salt and a few grinds of pepper. Toss to coat the pasta well. Remove from the heat. Throw in the mozzarella, sprinkle with the parmesan and dill and toss again. Sprinkle each serving with more parmesan.

"Summer herbs like parsley and basil are good with this pasta, too."

"*This is all the goodness of lasagna without the fuss!*"

Skillet Lasagna

Prep time: 30 min ★ Total time: 35 min ★ Serves: 4 to 6

½	teaspoon kosher salt, plus more to taste
2	tablespoons olive oil
1	onion, chopped
2	garlic cloves, minced

Black pepper, to taste

1	24-ounce jar marinara sauce
1	tablespoon Italian seasoning
14	lasagna noodles (not no-boil)
2	tablespoons salted butter
2	tablespoons grated parmesan cheese
1	cup diced fresh mozzarella cheese
½	cup fresh ricotta cheese

Small basil leaves, for topping

1 Bring a large pot of salted water to a boil. Heat the olive oil in a large skillet over medium-high heat. Add the onion and garlic and season with ½ teaspoon salt and a few grinds of pepper. Cook, stirring occasionally, until the onion is tender and lightly browned, about 8 minutes.

2 Add the marinara sauce, Italian seasoning and salt and pepper to taste. Stir, then reduce the heat to low and simmer until beginning to thicken, 10 to 15 minutes.

3 Meanwhile, break each lasagna noodle into 3 or 4 pieces (they don't have to be even). Add to the boiling water and cook, stirring frequently to prevent sticking, until tender, 8 to 10 minutes. Reserve 1 cup cooking water and then drain.

4 Add the butter and parmesan to the sauce and stir until it's all combined and melted. Throw in the cooked lasagna noodles and ½ cup of the reserved cooking water; stir to combine, adding the rest of the reserved cooking water as needed so the noodles are well coated and a bit saucy. Add the mozzarella and stir until softened but not fully melted.

5 Remove the skillet from the heat and dollop the ricotta all over the top. Sprinkle with basil leaves.

STEP BY STEP

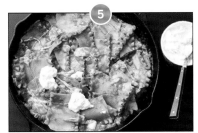

Tex-Mex Grain Bowls

Prep time: 30 min ★ Total time: 50 min ★ Serves: 4 to 6

1	pound carrots, peeled and cut into ½-inch pieces
1	pound parsnips, peeled and cut into ½-inch pieces
4	tablespoons vegetable oil
1½	teaspoons ground cumin
1	teaspoon chili powder
1¼	teaspoons kosher salt, plus more to taste
¼	teaspoon black pepper, plus more to taste
4	cups thinly sliced red cabbage

3	limes
1½	cups quinoa
1	cup fresh cilantro, chopped, plus more for topping
1	small onion, chopped
1	15-ounce can pinto beans, drained and rinsed
2	small avocados, sliced

Salsa, pickled jalapeños and crumbled Cotija cheese, for topping

1 Preheat the oven to 425˚. Toss the carrots, parsnips, 2 tablespoons vegetable oil, cumin, chili powder, 1 teaspoon salt and a few grinds of pepper on a rimmed baking sheet until well coated. Roast, stirring a few times, until tender and lightly browned, 25 to 30 minutes.

2 Meanwhile, add the cabbage to a medium bowl and squeeze 1 tablespoon lime juice over it. Add 1 tablespoon vegetable oil and ¼ teaspoon each salt and pepper, toss and set aside to soften.

3 Cook the quinoa as the label directs. Remove from the heat and fluff with a fork. Stir in the zest and juice of 1 lime and the cilantro.

4 Heat the remaining 1 tablespoon vegetable oil in a medium skillet over medium-high heat. Add the onion and a pinch each of salt and pepper. Cook, stirring, until softened, about 8 minutes.

5 Stir in the pinto beans. Cook until warmed through, about 2 minutes.

6 Divide the quinoa among bowls and top with the roasted veggies, bean mixture, cabbage and avocado. Top with salsa, pickled jalapeños, Cotija and more cilantro. Serve with lime wedges.

STEP BY STEP

"*Put out lots of different toppings and let everyone build a bowl!*"

"I love adding caramelized onions to just about everything!"

Penne with Cauliflower and Caramelized Onions

Prep time: 1 hr ★ Total time: 1 hr 10 min ★ Serves: 4 to 6

½ cup golden raisins
1 stick unsalted butter
1 large onion, thinly sliced
2½ teaspoons kosher salt, plus more for the pasta water
Black pepper, to taste
1 large head cauliflower, cut into florets
12 ounces penne
2 cups fresh parsley, roughly chopped
1 cup grated parmesan cheese, plus more for topping
½ cup toasted pine nuts
Grated zest of 1 lemon, plus 1 tablespoon lemon juice
3 garlic cloves, minced
¼ teaspoon crushed red pepper flakes

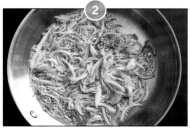

1. Cover the raisins with 1 cup hot water in a bowl and let sit until plump, about 15 minutes. Drain and set aside.
2. Meanwhile, melt 4 tablespoons butter in a large skillet over medium heat. Add the onion, 1 teaspoon salt and a few grinds of pepper and cook, stirring occasionally, until the onion is softened and a deep golden brown, 20 to 25 minutes. Remove from the pan and set aside.
3. Melt the remaining 4 tablespoons butter in the same skillet over medium heat. Add the cauliflower, ¾ cup water, 1 teaspoon salt and a few grinds of pepper and cook, tossing occasionally, until the water is evaporated and the cauliflower is tender and turning golden brown in some spots, 20 to 25 minutes.
4. While the cauliflower cooks, bring a large pot of salted water to a boil. Cook the pasta according to the package directions for al dente. Reserve 1½ cups cooking water, then drain.
5. Add the pasta, caramelized onion, parsley, parmesan, pine nuts, lemon zest, lemon juice, garlic, red pepper flakes, 1 cup reserved cooking water, the remaining ½ teaspoon salt and a few grinds of pepper to the skillet with the cauliflower. Cook, stirring constantly and adding more cooking water if needed, until the cheese is melted and the ingredients are well combined, 1 to 2 minutes. Gently fold in the raisins. Top the pasta with more parmesan, if desired.

Pasta with Ham, Leeks and Spinach

Prep time: 30 min ★ Total time: 30 min ★ Serves: 4 to 6

Kosher salt, to taste
12 ounces fettuccine
4   tablespoons salted butter
1   cup chopped ham steak (6 to 8 ounces)
3   leeks, thinly sliced
1¼ cups heavy cream
Black pepper, to taste
⅓   cup grated parmesan cheese, plus more for topping
1   10-ounce package baby spinach

1 Bring a large pot of salted water to a boil. Add the pasta and cook according to the package directions. Drain and set aside.

2 Meanwhile, melt the butter in a large skillet over medium-high heat. Add the ham and cook, stirring, until it starts to brown, about 3 minutes. Add the leeks and cook, stirring occasionally, until tender, about 8 minutes.

3 Reduce the heat to low, then pour in the heavy cream. Season with salt and pepper. Stir in the parmesan and then add the spinach. (You may need to add the spinach in batches until it wilts enough to add more.)

4 Add the hot pasta to the skillet and toss until everything is well coated and combined. Serve with more parmesan on top.

"I am a leek freak—I absolutely love them!"

"*Did you know you can make pesto out of zucchini? It's amazing!*"

Pasta with Zucchini Pesto

Prep time: 30 min ★ Total time: 30 min ★ Serves: 4 to 6

Kosher salt, to taste
1   pound mezzi rigatoni or other
     short pasta
1   pound green beans, cut into 1½-inch pieces
1   medium zucchini
¼   cup sliced almonds
2   garlic cloves

1   cup fresh parsley
½   cup fresh tarragon
⅓   cup plus 2 tablespoons olive oil
½   cup grated parmesan cheese, plus more for topping
Black pepper, to taste
1   pound yellow summer squash, cut into half-moons
¾   cup heavy cream

1. Bring a large pot of salted water to a boil. Add the pasta and cook according to the package directions, adding the green beans during the last 2 minutes. Reserve 1 cup cooking water, then drain the pasta and green beans and place in a large bowl.

2. Meanwhile, slice the zucchini in half lengthwise. Use a spoon to scrape out the seeds. Chop the zucchini into ½-inch pieces.

3. Make the pesto: Place the almonds and garlic in a food processor and pulse until finely chopped. Add the parsley, tarragon and zucchini and pulse until finely chopped. With the machine running, slowly drizzle in ⅓ cup olive oil and process until fairly smooth. Scrape into a bowl and mix in the parmesan and season with salt and pepper.

4. Heat the remaining 2 tablespoons olive oil in a large skillet over medium-high heat. Add the yellow squash, season with salt and pepper and cook, stirring, until browned, 4 to 5 minutes.

5. Add the heavy cream to the skillet and stir. Reduce the heat to low and let thicken slightly, about 2 minutes. Mix in the pesto until evenly distributed.

6. Add the pesto mixture to the pasta and green beans and toss, adding the reserved cooking water as needed to loosen. Serve with more parmesan for topping.

STEP BY STEP

Pasta Primavera with Peas and Mint

Prep time: 20 min ★ Total time: 30 min ★ Serves: 4 to 6

1	teaspoon kosher salt, plus more for cooking the pasta
1	pound fettuccine
8	ounces snap peas, trimmed and cut into thirds
1	cup frozen peas
1	cup grated parmesan cheese
½	cup heavy cream

Grated zest and juice of 1 lemon

½	cup fresh mint, chopped, plus more for topping
⅛	teaspoon black pepper

1. Bring a large pot of generously salted water to a boil. Add the pasta and cook according to the package directions for al dente.

2. With about 2 minutes of cooking time left, add the snap peas and frozen peas to the pot and cook until bright green and crisp-tender. Reserve 1 cup cooking water, then drain the pasta and peas.

3. Return the pasta and peas to the pot and place over medium heat. Add the parmesan, heavy cream and ⅓ cup of the pasta cooking water to the pot and cook, stirring constantly, until the parmesan melts and the heavy cream starts to thicken, about 2 minutes. Add more of the reserved cooking liquid if the pasta seems dry.

4. Add the lemon zest, lemon juice, mint, 1 teaspoon salt and the pepper; stir to combine. Serve in bowls and top with more mint.

STEP BY STEP

"Peas and mint are a perfect pair!"

"This is a great dish to make when fresh corn is abundant."

Rigatoni with Creamy Corn

Prep time: 30 min ★ Total time: 30 min ★ Serves: 4 to 6

1	teaspoon kosher salt, plus more for the pasta water
6	ears of corn, shucked
½	cup heavy cream
3	tablespoons salted butter, cut into pieces

Pinch of red pepper flakes

1	pound mezzi rigatoni (or other short pasta)
¾	cup grated parmesan cheese
¼	cup chopped fresh chives
¼	cup fresh parsley, chopped

1 Bring a large pot of salted water to a boil. Find a large heatproof bowl that will fit over the pasta pot like a double boiler. Slice the kernels off the cobs and put the kernels in the bowl. With the dull side of the knife (or with a butter knife), scrape each cob over the bowl to remove all the bits of kernel and creamy milk.

2 Add the heavy cream, butter, red pepper flakes and ½ teaspoon salt to the bowl.

3 Add the pasta to the boiling water and set the bowl with the corn mixture over the pasta pot.

4 Let the corn mixture warm, stirring occasionally, until the butter is melted and the pasta underneath is al dente, 10 to 12 minutes. Remove the bowl of corn. Reserve ½ cup of the pasta cooking water, then drain the pasta.

5 Add the hot pasta to the corn mixture. Sprinkle with the parmesan, chives and parsley and toss well, adding the reserved cooking water a little at a time if the pasta seems dry. Season with the remaining ½ teaspoon salt.

STEP BY STEP

Baked Spinach Ravioli with Pesto Cream Sauce

Prep time: 25 min ★ Total time: 55 min ★ Serves: 4 to 6

Kosher salt, for the water

2	10-ounce packages fresh or frozen spinach ravioli
1	5-ounce bag baby spinach
2	tablespoons salted butter
2	tablespoons all-purpose flour
2	cups half-and-half
1	7-ounce container pesto
2	cups grated whole-milk mozzarella cheese (about 8 ounces)
¼	cup freshly grated parmesan cheese

1 Preheat the oven to 400°. Bring a large pot of salted water to a boil. Add the ravioli and cook according to the package directions. Drain the ravioli.

2 Combine the spinach and ravioli in a 9-by-13-inch baking dish and gently toss to combine.

3 Melt the butter in a medium saucepan over medium-low heat. Whisk in the flour and cook, whisking constantly, until golden, 2 to 3 minutes (don't let the flour burn). Slowly whisk in the half-and-half until smooth. Cook, whisking occasionally, until thickened, about 7 minutes.

4 Reduce the heat to low. Whisk in the pesto until just heated through, about 1 minute.

5 Pour the pesto cream sauce over the spinach and ravioli. Spread with a spoon, making sure all the ravioli are coated. Sprinkle with the mozzarella and parmesan. Bake until the sauce is bubbling and the edges are browned, about 25 minutes. Let cool 5 minutes before serving.

STEP BY STEP

"This is such a simple dinner. Use any kind of ravioli you like!"

"This one is for all the pepper lovers out there!"

Six Pepper Pasta

Prep time: 30 min ★ Total time: 30 min ★ Serves: 4 to 6

Kosher salt, to taste
1   pound fettuccine
2   tablespoons salted butter
2   tablespoons olive oil
3   garlic cloves, minced
1   onion, diced
6   multicolored baby bell peppers, sliced crosswise into rounds
1   red bell pepper, seeded and thinly sliced
1   orange bell pepper, seeded and thinly sliced
1   jalapeño pepper, seeded and thinly sliced
1   poblano pepper, seeded and thinly sliced
Black pepper, to taste
½   cup silver tequila
2   cups vegetable broth
1   cup heavy cream
3   tablespoons adobo sauce (from a can of chipotles),
      plus more if needed
¼   cup fresh cilantro, chopped

1. Bring a large pot of salted water to a boil. Add the pasta and cook according to the package instructions. Drain and set aside.

2. Meanwhile, heat the butter and olive oil in a large high-sided skillet over medium-high heat. Add the garlic and onion and cook, stirring, until the onion begins to soften and slightly brown, about 3 minutes. Add the baby pepper rounds, reserving a few for topping. Add the red and orange bell peppers, plus the jalapeño and poblano; season with a pinch each of salt and pepper. Cook, stirring, until the peppers begin to soften and darken, 3 to 4 minutes.

3. Transfer the vegetables to a plate, then return the skillet to medium-high heat and allow it to warm up. Remove from the heat; pour in the tequila. Return to medium-high heat and cook the tequila for 1 minute, scraping pepper bits from the bottom of the pan. Add the broth and bring to a simmer, then cook until reduced slightly, 3 to 5 minutes. Reduce the heat to medium low and pour in the heavy cream. Add the adobo sauce, stirring constantly. Cook until starting to thicken, 4 to 5 minutes.

4. Return the vegetables to the skillet, along with any collected juices from the plate. Cook, stirring, until the mixture is hot, 1 to 2 minutes. Season with salt, pepper and more adobo sauce, if needed.

5. Add the pasta to the sauce and toss. Top each serving of pasta with the cilantro and reserved baby pepper rings.

Mac and Cheese
with Everything Bagel Topping

Prep time: 25 min ★ Total time: 50 min ★ Serves: 6

3	tablespoons salted butter, plus more for the ramekins
½	teaspoon kosher salt, plus more to taste
3	cups elbow macaroni
3	tablespoons all-purpose flour
1	teaspoon mustard powder
½	teaspoon paprika
½	teaspoon seasoned salt, plus more to taste
½	teaspoon black pepper
2	cups whole milk
1	large egg
4	ounces cream cheese
3	cups grated mild cheddar cheese
2	cups bagel chips, crushed into small crumbs

Everything bagel seasoning, for sprinkling

1 Preheat the oven to 350°. Butter six 8-ounce ramekins or mini baking dishes and place on a rimmed baking sheet. Bring a pot of salted water to a boil. Add the pasta and cook until softened but still too firm to eat, about 5 minutes. Drain the pasta.

2 Melt the butter in a large pot over medium-low heat. Sprinkle in the flour and cook, whisking constantly, until golden, about 5 minutes. (Don't let it burn!) Add the mustard powder, paprika, ½ teaspoon salt, the seasoned salt and pepper. Pour in the milk, whisking until smooth. Cook, whisking, until thickened, about 5 minutes. Reduce the heat to low.

3 Beat the egg in a large bowl. Slowly pour ¼ cup of the hot sauce into the beaten egg, whisking constantly. Pour the egg mixture into the pot with the remaining sauce, whisking constantly. Add the cream cheese and 2½ cups cheddar; stir to melt. Add more salt and seasoned salt to taste, but keep in mind that the topping will be salty.

4 Add the pasta to the cheese sauce and stir to combine.

5 Divide the pasta among the ramekins. Top with the bagel chips and sprinkle with the remaining ½ cup cheddar and everything seasoning. Bake until bubbly and golden, 20 to 25 minutes.

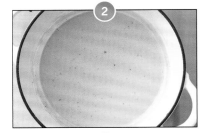

"*Everything seasoning is... everything! It's especially good on mac and cheese.*"

"Italian sausage and broccoli rabe are a match made in pasta heaven."

Rigatoni with Broccoli Rabe and Sausage

Prep time: 35 min ★ Total time: 35 min ★ Serves: 4 to 6

Kosher salt, to taste
1   pound rigatoni
3   tablespoons olive oil
1   large bunch broccoli rabe,
     trimmed and cut into 2-inch pieces
1   pound sweet Italian sausage, casings removed
1   large onion, thinly sliced
2   tablespoons tomato paste
4   garlic cloves, thinly sliced
¼   teaspoon red pepper flakes
½   cup fresh parsley, chopped
½   cup grated pecorino romano cheese, plus more for topping

1 Bring a large pot of salted water to a boil. Add the pasta and cook according to the package directions for al dente, adding the broccoli rabe in the last 4 minutes of cooking. Reserve 2½ cups of the cooking water, then drain the pasta and broccoli rabe.

2 Meanwhile, heat a large dutch oven over medium heat and add the olive oil. When the oil is hot, add the sausage and cook, breaking it up with a wooden spoon, until browned, about 4 minutes. Add the onion and cook, stirring occasionally, until softened, about 5 minutes.

3 Add the tomato paste, garlic and red pepper flakes to the pot and cook, stirring, until sizzling, 30 seconds. Add 2 cups of the reserved cooking water, bring to a simmer and cook until reduced by half, 5 to 6 minutes.

4 Add the pasta, broccoli rabe and parsley to the sauce and toss to coat, adding more of the reserved cooking water if the pasta seems dry. Season with salt, if needed. Remove from the heat, sprinkle with the grated cheese and toss well. Top each serving with more grated cheese.

Caprese Chicken Pasta

Prep time: 20 min ★ Total time: 25 min ★ Serves: 4 to 6

Kosher salt, to taste
1   pound rigatoni
¼   cup olive oil
⅓   cup panko breadcrumbs
⅔   cup grated parmesan cheese
1   pound skinless, boneless chicken
     breasts, cut into 1-inch chunks

Black pepper, to taste
2   pints grape or cherry tomatoes
3   garlic cloves, thinly sliced
Pinch of red pepper flakes
8   ounces bocconcini (mini mozzarella
     balls), halved
½   cup fresh basil, torn

1 Bring a large pot of salted water to a boil. Add the pasta and cook according to the package directions for al dente. Reserve 2 cups of the cooking water, then drain the pasta.

2 Meanwhile, heat 1 tablespoon olive oil in a large skillet over medium-low heat. Stir in the panko and cook, stirring, until golden, 1 to 2 minutes. Scrape into a bowl to cool, then stir in ⅓ cup parmesan and set aside.

3 Wipe out the skillet. Add 2 tablespoons olive oil and heat over medium-high heat. Add the chicken and season with salt and pepper. Cook, turning, until browned on all sides, about 3 minutes; remove to a plate.

4 Add the remaining 1 tablespoon olive oil to the skillet over medium-high heat. Add the tomatoes and cook until blistered, about 1 minute. Reduce the heat to medium, add the garlic and red pepper flakes and cook until the garlic just begins to turn golden, about 30 seconds. Add 1½ cups of the reserved cooking water and bring to a boil. Lower the heat and simmer until the liquid is reduced by half and the tomatoes begin to burst, about 3 minutes.

5 Return the chicken to the skillet and cook through, about 2 more minutes.

6 Add the pasta to the skillet and toss to coat, adding some of the remaining pasta water if needed. Remove from the heat; sprinkle with the remaining ⅓ cup parmesan. Add the bocconcini and basil, season with salt and pepper and toss well. Sprinkle with the panko mixture just before serving.

STEP BY STEP

"Caprese is such a magical combination of flavors and textures!"

Poultry

"Quesadillas were my number-one pregnancy craving!"

Lime Chicken Quesadillas

Prep time: 45 min ★ Total time: 1 hr 30 min ★ Serves: 4 to 6

1	pound skinless, boneless chicken breasts
4	cups low-sodium chicken broth
½	cup fresh lime juice (from about 6 limes)
2	cups fresh cilantro
6	garlic cloves, chopped
2	jalapeño peppers, sliced
2	teaspoons kosher salt
⅔	cup light olive oil
2	cups shredded cheddar cheese (about 8 ounces)
2	tablespoons canned chopped green chiles
3	tablespoons salted butter, softened
12	small flour tortillas

1 Put the chicken in a medium saucepan. Add the broth and enough water to cover by 1 inch. Bring to a boil, then reduce the heat so that the broth just simmers. Partially cover and cook until a meat thermometer inserted into the chicken reaches 155° to 160°, 20 to 30 minutes, depending on the thickness of the chicken.

2 Remove the chicken to a cutting board (discard the broth). Let cool slightly, then shred with 2 forks.

3 Combine the lime juice, cilantro, garlic, jalapeños and salt in a blender. Pulse to get everything started; then, with the blender running, drizzle in the olive oil and blend until smooth.

4 Preheat the oven to 425°. Combine the chicken in a large bowl with ½ cup of the cilantro sauce, the cheddar and chiles.

5 Put 1 tablespoon butter on each of 2 baking sheets and put them in the oven. Spread the remaining 1 tablespoon butter on 6 tortillas. Divide the chicken mixture among the 6 unbuttered tortillas, spreading it almost to the edges. Top with the buttered tortillas, buttered-side up, and press together.

6 By now the butter on the baking sheets should be melted. Spread it out with a spatula. Put 3 quesadillas buttered-side up on each baking sheet. Bake until golden brown on the bottom, about 4 minutes. Flip and bake until golden on the other side, about 2 more minutes. Cut the quesadillas into wedges. Serve with the remaining cilantro sauce.

STEP BY STEP

Roast Jerk Chicken

Prep time: 30 min ★ Total time: 2 hr (plus marinating) ★ Serves: 4 to 6

¼ cup olive oil
2 tablespoons lime juice (from about 1 lime)
2 tablespoons soy sauce
1 tablespoon ground allspice
1 tablespoon packed dark brown sugar
1 tablespoon fresh thyme
2 teaspoons kosher salt
2 teaspoons black pepper
1 teaspoon ground cinnamon
1 teaspoon ground nutmeg
3 garlic cloves, crushed
1 bunch scallions, roughly chopped
1 jalapeño pepper, chopped
1 1½-inch piece fresh ginger, peeled and chopped
1 4- to 5-pound whole chicken
Mixed greens and vinaigrette, for serving

1 Combine the olive oil, lime juice, soy sauce, allspice, brown sugar, thyme, salt, pepper, cinnamon, nutmeg, garlic, scallions, jalapeño and ginger in a food processor. Blend until smooth.

2 Pat the chicken dry and place it on a rack set on a rimmed baking sheet. Rub the jerk marinade all over the chicken, making sure to get a good amount under the skin of the breast and thighs. Refrigerate, uncovered, for at least 30 minutes and preferably overnight.

3 Preheat the oven to 425°. Remove the chicken from the refrigerator. Tent loosely with foil (try not to let the foil touch the skin of the chicken). Roast for 30 minutes, then uncover and roast until a thermometer inserted into the thickest part of the thigh reaches 160°, 35 to 40 more minutes.

4 Let the chicken rest for 20 minutes, then carve and serve with mixed greens tossed with vinaigrette.

STEP BY STEP

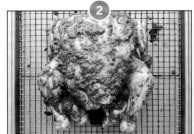

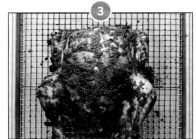

"You can marinate the chicken the night before, so dinner is extra easy the next day!"

"*Throw in whatever veggies you have on hand. Anything goes!*"

Chicken–Snow Pea Stir-Fry

Prep time: 35 min ★ Total time: 25 min ★ Serves: 4 to 6

½   cup low-sodium soy sauce, plus more for serving
3   tablespoons sherry
2   tablespoons packed brown sugar
2   tablespoons cornstarch
1   tablespoon minced fresh ginger
1½ pounds skinless, boneless chicken thighs,
    trimmed of fat and cut into ¾-inch pieces
3   tablespoons peanut oil
8   ounces snow peas, trimmed
Kosher salt, to taste
Cooked white rice, for serving
Red pepper flakes, for topping
Chopped roasted cashews, for topping (optional)

① Mix the soy sauce, sherry, brown sugar, cornstarch
   and ginger in a small bowl. Pour about a third of the
   mixture over the chicken in a large bowl and toss with
   your hands; set aside. Reserve the remaining liquid.
② Heat the peanut oil in a large cast-iron skillet or wok
   over high heat. Add the snow peas and stir-fry for
   45 seconds. Remove to a plate and set aside.
③ Let the skillet get very hot again. Using tongs, add
   the chicken mixture, leaving most of the marinade in
   the bowl. Spread out the chicken as you add it to the
   pan but do not stir for a good minute so the chicken
   gets nice and brown on the bottom. Then flip the
   chicken and cook through, tossing occasionally,
   5 to 6 minutes.
④ Add ½ cup water, the reserved marinade and the
   snow peas to the skillet. Cook over high heat, stirring,
   for 30 seconds, then turn off the heat. (The sauce will
   thicken as it sits.) Season with salt only if it needs it.
   Serve over rice and top with red pepper flakes and
   cashews, if desired.

STEP BY STEP

Sheet-Pan Curried Chicken

Prep time: 15 min ★ Total time: 1 hr ★ Serves: 4 to 6

½	cup red curry paste
1	heaping tablespoon packed dark brown sugar
3	tablespoons vegetable oil, plus more for the pan
1	pound green beans, trimmed
1	pound carrots, halved lengthwise and cut into 1½-inch pieces
2½	teaspoons kosher salt
12	skin-on chicken drumsticks
⅓	cup fresh cilantro, roughly chopped

Cooked white rice, for serving
Lime wedges, for serving (optional)

1 Position a rack in the lower third of the oven and preheat to 425°. Combine the curry paste, brown sugar and vegetable oil in a small bowl.

2 Put the green beans and carrots in a large bowl and toss with a little less than half of the curry mixture and ½ teaspoon salt. Spread out on an oiled rimmed baking sheet.

3 Add the chicken and 2 teaspoons salt to the empty bowl, add the remaining curry mixture and toss. Add to the pan, nestling the chicken in the vegetables.

4 Roast until the vegetables are tender and a thermometer inserted into the chicken (without touching the bone!) registers 170°, 40 to 45 minutes. Turn the vegetables and chicken halfway through cooking to prevent them from getting too dark on the bottom. Scrape the chicken, vegetables and any browned bits from the pan into a large serving dish and sprinkle with the cilantro. Serve with rice and lime wedges, if desired.

STEP BY STEP

"Red curry paste gives the chicken and veggies a kick."

"*This soup is meaty, hearty and satisfying!*"

Turkey Burger Soup

Prep time: 25 min ★ Total time: 50 min ★ Serves: 4 to 6

2	tablespoons olive oil
1½	pounds ground turkey
1	small onion, diced
2	garlic cloves, minced
1	14.5-ounce can whole peeled tomatoes, crushed by hand
2	cups low-sodium chicken broth, plus more as needed
1	heaping tablespoon tomato paste
1	teaspoon dried parsley
¼	teaspoon ground oregano
½	teaspoon kosher salt, plus more to taste
¼	teaspoon black pepper, plus more to taste

Pinch of cayenne pepper

2	carrots, peeled and sliced
2	large red potatoes, cut into 1-inch chunks
1	large red bell pepper, chopped
8	ounces green beans, cut into pieces

1 Heat the olive oil in a large dutch oven over high heat. Add the turkey, onion and garlic and cook, stirring, until the turkey is browned, about 8 minutes.

2 Add the tomatoes and their juices, the chicken broth, tomato paste, parsley, oregano, salt, black pepper and cayenne. Stir to combine.

3 Throw in the carrots, potatoes and bell pepper. Stir everything together, then bring the mixture to a boil. Reduce the heat, cover and simmer, stirring occasionally, until the potatoes are almost tender, 10 to 15 minutes.

4 Stir in the green beans, then cover and cook until the beans are crisp-tender and the potatoes are tender but not mushy, another 4 or 5 minutes. If the soup is too thick for your taste, just splash in more broth until it's the consistency you like. Season to taste before serving.

STEP BY STEP

Slow-Cooker White Chicken Chili

Prep time: 20 min ★ Total time: 7 hr 50 min ★ Serves: 4 to 6

3	skinless, boneless chicken breasts (about 1½ pounds)
1	tablespoon ground cumin
1	tablespoon ground coriander
2	teaspoons dried oregano
½	teaspoon paprika
½	teaspoon crushed red pepper flakes
1	teaspoon kosher salt

Black pepper, to taste

2	15-ounce cans cannellini beans, drained and rinsed
2	4-ounce cans chopped green chiles
2	garlic cloves, minced
2	cups low-sodium chicken broth
½	cup heavy cream
2	tablespoons masa harina
1	10-ounce bag frozen corn

Grated Monterey Jack cheese and chopped avocado, for topping
Lime wedges, for serving

1 Put the chicken breasts in a 6- to 8-quart slow cooker. Mix the cumin, coriander, oregano, paprika, red pepper flakes, salt and a few grinds of pepper in a small bowl. Sprinkle the spices over the chicken.

2 Add the beans, green chiles, garlic and chicken broth to the slow cooker and stir it all around. Cover and cook on low until the chicken is cooked through and easy to shred, 7 to 8 hours.

3 Remove the chicken to a medium bowl and shred with 2 forks.

4 Combine the heavy cream and masa harina in a small bowl. Mix until smooth.

5 Return the chicken to the slow cooker along with the masa mixture and corn. Cover and cook on low until the chili is thickened and the corn is warmed through, about 30 minutes. Ladle the chili into bowls and top with cheese and avocado. Serve with lime wedges.

STEP BY STEP

"Dream dinner: Throw everything in a slow cooker. Turn on. Go live life."

"The Instant Pot is perfect for this dish—it cuts the cooking time in half!"

Instant Pot Chicken Cacciatore

Prep time: 30 min ★ Total time: 1 hr 25 min ★ Serves: 4 to 6

8	skin-on, bone-in chicken thighs
½	teaspoon kosher salt, plus more to taste
½	teaspoon black pepper, plus more to taste
½	cup all-purpose flour
2	tablespoons olive oil
⅓	cup dry white wine or low-sodium chicken broth
2	tablespoons tomato paste
½	teaspoon red pepper flakes
½	teaspoon ground thyme
¼	teaspoon ground turmeric
5	garlic cloves, minced
2	bell peppers (any color), sliced
1	medium onion, halved and sliced
1	14.5-ounce can diced tomatoes
8	ounces cremini mushrooms, sliced
12	ounces wide egg noodles

Green salad, for serving

1 Sprinkle both sides of the chicken with the salt and pepper. Dredge in the flour.

2 Set a 6-quart Instant Pot to sauté and heat the olive oil. Working in 2 batches, add the chicken, skin-side down, and cook until browned, 6 to 8 minutes per side. Remove to a plate.

3 Add the wine or broth, tomato paste, red pepper flakes, thyme and turmeric to the pot and cook until you no longer smell the alcohol, 2 to 3 minutes. Add the garlic, bell peppers, onion, tomatoes and mushrooms; season with salt and pepper. Toss to coat the vegetables. Place the chicken on top.

4 Lock the lid, making sure the steam valve is in the sealing position. Set to pressure cook on high for 20 minutes. After the cycle is complete, carefully release the steam manually. Be careful of any remaining steam and remove the lid. Transfer the chicken to a plate. Set the pot to sauté on high and cook the sauce until thickened, 10 minutes.

5 Meanwhile, bring a large pot of water to a boil and cook the noodles according to the package directions. Drain.

6 Toss the noodles, vegetables and sauce in a large bowl. Serve with the chicken and salad.

STEP BY STEP

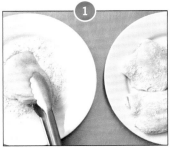

Greek Chicken Kebabs

Prep time: 40 min ★ Total time: 1 hr 10 min ★ Serves: 4 to 6

TZATZIKI
1 seedless cucumber
2 cups plain Greek yogurt
¼ cup fresh dill, chopped
Grated zest of 1 lemon, plus
      2 tablespoons lemon juice
1 small garlic clove, grated
Kosher salt and black pepper, to taste

KEBABS
1 tablespoon garlic powder
1 tablespoon lemon-pepper seasoning
2 teaspoons fennel seeds, crushed
2 teaspoons dried oregano
1½ teaspoons kosher salt
¼ cup vegetable oil
6 skinless, boneless chicken thighs
      (about 2¼ pounds), cut into thirds
1½ sweet onions, cut into wedges
1 large zucchini, thickly sliced
4 to 6 pieces pita bread, cut into quarters

1 Soak 12 wooden skewers in water for at least 30 minutes. Preheat a grill to medium high. For the tzatziki: Slice the cucumber in half lengthwise and use a spoon to scrape out the seeds, if there are any. Grate the cucumber onto paper towels; squeeze out the excess moisture. Mix the yogurt, dill, lemon zest, lemon juice and garlic in a bowl. Add the grated cucumber and season with salt and pepper.

2 For the kebabs: Combine the garlic powder, lemon-pepper, fennel seeds, oregano and salt in a large bowl. Whisk in 3 tablespoons vegetable oil. Add the chicken and toss to evenly coat.

3 Toss the onions and zucchini with the remaining 1 tablespoon vegetable oil in a bowl and season with salt and pepper. Thread the chicken, onion and zucchini onto the skewers.

4 Grill the kebabs, covered, turning occasionally, until the chicken is cooked through, 15 to 20 minutes. Warm the pitas on the grill, about 2 minutes per side. Serve the kebabs with the pita and tzatziki.

"Be sure to soak wooden skewers in water before grilling so they don't scorch."

"This meal has all the goodness of a loaded baked potato!"

Loaded Chicken and Tater Tots

Prep time: 30 min ★ Total time: 40 min ★ Serves: 4 to 6

1	pound frozen Tater Tots
1	head broccoli, cut into florets
2	tablespoons olive oil

Kosher salt and black pepper, to taste

6	slices bacon
1	pound chicken tenders
1½	teaspoons smoked paprika
½	teaspoon garlic powder
1	cup shredded sharp cheddar cheese

Chopped fresh chives, for topping
Sour cream, for serving

1. Preheat the oven to 450°. Spread the Tater Tots on a rimmed baking sheet and bake until crisp and golden, about 25 minutes. Meanwhile, toss the broccoli with the olive oil on a second baking sheet; season with salt and pepper. After the tots have baked about 5 minutes, put the broccoli in the oven and roast, switching the pans halfway through, until charred and tender, about 20 minutes. The tots and broccoli should be finished around the same time.

2. Meanwhile, cook the bacon in a large cast-iron skillet over medium heat, turning, until crisp, 7 to 8 minutes. Drain on paper towels and break into pieces. Pour off all but 2 tablespoons bacon fat from the pan.

3. Toss the chicken in a large bowl with the smoked paprika and garlic powder. Season with salt and pepper.

4. Heat the bacon fat in the skillet over medium-high heat. Add the chicken and cook until browned, 1 to 2 minutes per side. (It doesn't need to be cooked through—it'll finish cooking in the oven.)

5. Combine the tots and broccoli on 1 baking sheet, spreading them in an even layer. Arrange the chicken on top and sprinkle with the cheddar. Bake until the cheese is browned and bubbly and the chicken is cooked through, 3 to 5 minutes. Top with the bacon and chives and serve with sour cream.

Greek-Style Turkey Burgers

Prep time: 40 min ★ Total time: 40 min ★ Serves: 6

1	medium seedless cucumber
1½	cups whole-milk plain Greek yogurt
2	tablespoons olive oil, plus more for brushing
1	tablespoon chopped fresh dill
1	tablespoon fresh lemon juice
1	small garlic clove, finely chopped
1	teaspoon kosher salt

Black pepper, to taste

1	red onion
2	pounds ground turkey
1	large egg yolk
1	teaspoon dried oregano
6	pitas
½	head Boston lettuce
1	4-ounce package crumbled feta cheese (about ¾ cup)

Potato chips, for serving

1 Preheat the oven to 250°. For the tzatziki: Grate ½ cucumber onto a clean kitchen towel and wring dry.

2 Combine the grated cucumber with the yogurt, olive oil, dill, lemon juice, garlic, ½ teaspoon salt and a few grinds of pepper in a medium bowl. Refrigerate while you make the burgers.

3 For the burgers: Grate ½ red onion and combine with the turkey, egg yolk, oregano, remaining ½ teaspoon salt and a few grinds of pepper in a large bowl. Mix with your hands, then form into six ½-inch-thick patties. Place on a sheet of parchment.

4 Put the pitas on a baking sheet and keep warm in the oven.

5 Heat a large cast-iron or other nonstick skillet over medium-high heat and brush with olive oil. Add 3 patties and cook until no longer pink in the center, 4 to 5 minutes per side. Transfer to a separate baking sheet and keep warm in the oven. Wipe out the pan, brush with more olive oil and repeat with the remaining patties.

6 Cut off the tops of the pitas. Chop the remaining ½ cucumber and slice the remaining ½ red onion. Spread some tzatziki inside each pita. Fill each with lettuce, a patty, cucumber, red onion and feta. Serve with chips.

STEP BY STEP

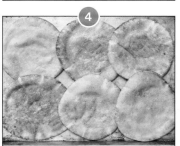

"I put all the best parts of a Greek salad on a burger—including lots of feta!"

"BBQ chicken is a summer staple on the ranch. The Instant Pot makes it so easy!"

Instant Pot BBQ Chicken Grain Bowls

Prep time: 45 min ★ Total time: 1 hr 20 min ★ Serves: 4 to 6

2   pounds skinless, boneless chicken thighs
2   garlic cloves, sliced
1   medium onion, sliced
1   teaspoon kosher salt
Black pepper, to taste
1¼   cups barbecue sauce, plus more for topping
1   cup quinoa
1   avocado, sliced
1   large mango, cut into small cubes
1   jalapeño pepper, thinly sliced (remove seeds for less heat)
4   radishes, thinly sliced
Chopped fresh cilantro, for topping

1. Combine the chicken, garlic, onion, ½ teaspoon salt, a few grinds of pepper and ¼ cup water in a 6-quart Instant Pot. Pour in the barbecue sauce.

2. Put on and lock the lid, making sure the steam valve is in the sealing position. Set the pot to pressure-cook on high for 15 minutes. When the time is up, let the pressure release naturally for 10 minutes. Carefully turn the steam valve to the venting position and release the remaining pressure. Unlock and remove the lid, being careful of any remaining steam.

3. Transfer the chicken to a large bowl and shred with 2 forks. Set the Instant Pot to sauté on high and cook the sauce until thickened, about 10 minutes. Add the sauce to the chicken and toss.

4. Meanwhile, bring 2¼ cups water to a boil in a medium saucepan. Add the quinoa, the remaining ½ teaspoon salt and a few grinds of pepper and return to a boil. Reduce the heat to low; simmer until the quinoa is tender and the water is absorbed, about 20 minutes.

5. Scoop ½ cup quinoa into each bowl. Top with the chicken, avocado, mango, jalapeño, radishes and cilantro. Drizzle with more barbecue sauce.

Pretzel-Crusted Chicken with Broccoli

Prep time: 50 min ★ Total time: 55 min ★ Serves: 6

6   chicken cutlets (about 1½ pounds)
1½ teaspoons kosher salt, plus more to taste
1½ teaspoons black pepper
1   cup spicy brown mustard
1   cup mayonnaise
½   cup honey

½   cup all-purpose flour
5   cups pretzel twists, finely crushed
    (about 2 cups crushed)
4   tablespoons salted butter
¼   cup olive oil
2   bunches broccoli, cut into florets

1 Preheat the oven to 200°. Set a wire rack on a baking sheet. Season the chicken cutlets on both sides with salt and pepper, using about 1 teaspoon of each total.

2 Stir together the mustard, mayonnaise and honey in a small bowl. Remove 1 cup of the mixture to a shallow bowl, reserving the rest for serving.

3 Place the flour in another shallow bowl. Spread the pretzels on a plate. Coat each piece of chicken in the flour, then dunk in the honey-mustard mixture and then coat in the pretzels. Set on a large plate.

4 Heat 2 tablespoons each butter and olive oil in a large nonstick skillet over medium-low heat until the butter is melted and the oil is hot. Add 3 pieces of the crusted chicken and cook until golden brown and cooked through, 2 to 3 minutes per side. Remove the chicken to the rack and place in the oven.

5 Repeat with the remaining butter, oil and chicken. Add the chicken to the pan in the oven to keep warm.

6 Bring 1 inch of water to a simmer in a large saucepan fitted with a steamer basket. Add the broccoli, cover and cook until bright green and just tender, 8 to 10 minutes. Season with the remaining ½ teaspoon each salt and pepper. Serve the chicken and broccoli with the reserved honey-mustard sauce for dipping.

STEP BY STEP

"Crushed pretzels make the best crust—they're salty and crunchy!"

"We have a similar salad on the menu at The Merc. The berries are so refreshing."

Grilled Chicken Salad with Blue Cheese and Berries

Prep time: 40 min ★ Total time: 50 min ★ Serves: 4 to 6

1   teaspoon dried dill
2½ teaspoons sweet paprika
1½ teaspoons kosher salt, plus more to taste
Black pepper, to taste
1½ pounds skinless, boneless chicken breasts
⅓   cup plus 2 tablespoons olive oil
½   cup pecans, chopped
4   cups cubed brioche or challah
    bread (about half of a 14-ounce loaf)
2   tablespoons salted butter, melted

3   tablespoons red wine vinegar
2   teaspoons honey
1   teaspoon dijon mustard
1   6-ounce container raspberries
1   8-ounce bag mixed baby greens
1   6-ounce container blackberries
1   6-ounce container blueberries
4   ounces gorgonzola dolce cheese,
    crumbled
¼   cup chopped fresh chives

1 Preheat the oven to 325°. Preheat a grill or grill pan to medium high. Combine the dill, 2 teaspoons paprika, 1 teaspoon salt and a few grinds of pepper in a small bowl. Put the chicken on a baking sheet and rub with the spice mix. Brush with 2 tablespoons olive oil. Let sit while you prepare the salad.

2 Spread the pecans on a parchment-lined baking sheet and bake until toasted, 6 to 7 minutes. Transfer to a bowl to cool.

3 Toss the bread cubes in a large bowl with the melted butter and remaining ½ teaspoon paprika. Spread on the same baking sheet. Bake, tossing once, until crisp, about 10 minutes. Season with salt and let cool.

4 Grill the chicken until marked and cooked through, about 5 minutes per side. Remove to a cutting board.

5 For the dressing: Combine the vinegar, honey, mustard, ⅓ cup raspberries, the remaining ½ teaspoon salt and a few grinds of pepper in a large bowl. Mash the berries with a fork. Add the remaining ⅓ cup olive oil and whisk to make a smooth, thick dressing.

6 Slice the chicken and add to the dressing along with the greens and all the remaining berries. Season with salt and pepper and toss. Sprinkle with the pecans, croutons, gorgonzola and chives. Toss gently.

STEP BY STEP

Nashville Hot Chicken Plate

Prep time: 1 hr ★ Total time: 2 hr ★ Serves: 4 to 6

CHICKEN

4	skin-on, bone-in chicken breasts, halved crosswise
2	tablespoons plus 1½ teaspoons kosher salt
1	tablespoon plus 1½ teaspoons black pepper

Vegetable oil, for frying

2	cups all-purpose flour
6	tablespoons cayenne pepper
1½	cups buttermilk
2	tablespoons hot sauce
2	large eggs
2	tablespoons packed light brown sugar
1	teaspoon paprika
½	teaspoon garlic powder

Dinner rolls and pickle slices, for serving

SLAW

1	cup buttermilk
½	cup mayonnaise
1	tablespoon granulated sugar
2	teaspoons white vinegar
½	teaspoon kosher salt
1	teaspoon black pepper
2	carrots, shredded
1	head green cabbage, shredded
¼	cup fresh parsley, finely chopped

1. For the chicken: Toss the chicken with 2 tablespoons salt and 1 tablespoon black pepper. Cover and refrigerate at least 1 hour and up to overnight.

2. For the slaw: Combine the buttermilk, mayonnaise, granulated sugar, vinegar, salt and pepper in a large bowl. Add the carrots, cabbage and parsley and toss. Refrigerate until ready to serve.

3. Fry the chicken: Heat 2½ inches of vegetable oil in a large dutch oven over medium heat until a deep-fry thermometer registers 325°. Whisk the flour with 1 tablespoon cayenne, ½ teaspoon salt and ½ teaspoon black pepper in a large bowl. Whisk the buttermilk, hot sauce and eggs in another bowl. Dredge the chicken in the flour, then dip in the buttermilk mixture, then in the flour again, shaking off any excess. Place on a large plate.

4. Fry 3 or 4 pieces of chicken until golden brown and the internal temperature reaches 165°, 15 to 18 minutes. Remove to a rack set on a baking sheet. Repeat with the remaining chicken.

5. Carefully ladle 1 cup of the frying oil into a heatproof measuring cup. Whisk in the brown sugar, paprika, garlic powder, remaining 5 tablespoons cayenne and 1 teaspoon each salt and pepper. Pour over the chicken, turning to coat. Serve with the slaw, rolls and pickles.

"*This chicken has a serious kick! But don't let that scare you away.*"

"The caramelized glaze sends the flavor of this meal into the stratosphere!"

Sheet-Pan Teriyaki Chicken

Prep time: 15 min ★ Total time: 35 min ★ Serves: 4 to 6

12	assorted baby bell peppers, stemmed and halved lengthwise
1	bunch asparagus, trimmed and cut into 2-inch pieces
1	head broccoli, cut into small florets
1	bunch scallions, halved lengthwise and cut crosswise into 1-inch pieces
1	medium red onion, cut into large chunks, layers separated
1½	cups teriyaki glaze
8	skinless, boneless chicken thighs
1	lime

Sesame seeds and chopped fresh cilantro, for topping

1. Preheat the oven to 400°. Line a baking sheet with foil. Put the baby bell peppers, asparagus, broccoli, scallions and red onion on the baking sheet and drizzle with ¾ cup of the teriyaki glaze. Toss until well coated. Split the remaining ¾ cup of teriyaki glaze between 2 bowls.
2. Arrange the chicken thighs on top of the veggies and brush with 1 of the bowls of glaze.
3. Bake until the chicken is cooked through, about 20 minutes. Brush the chicken with the other bowl of teriyaki glaze, then turn on the broiler and broil until the sauce starts to caramelize on the chicken, 3 to 4 minutes. Watch it carefully to make sure it doesn't burn!
4. Grate the lime zest all over the chicken and veggies. Sprinkle with sesame seeds and cilantro.

STEP BY STEP

Chicken Caesar Milanese

Prep time: 40 min ★ Total time: 40 min ★ Serves: 4 to 6

DRESSING

2 tablespoons dijon mustard
1 tablespoon red wine vinegar
1 teaspoon Worcestershire sauce
4 anchovy fillets
2 garlic cloves
Juice of ½ lemon
½ cup olive oil
¼ cup grated parmesan cheese, plus more for serving
¼ teaspoon kosher salt
1 teaspoon black pepper, plus more to taste

CHICKEN

3 skinless, boneless chicken breasts (about 1½ pounds)
¼ cup whole milk
1 tablespoon dijon mustard
3 large eggs
½ cup all-purpose flour
Kosher salt and black pepper, to taste
1 cup seasoned breadcrumbs
½ cup grated parmesan cheese
⅓ cup olive oil, plus more as needed
3 romaine lettuce hearts, chopped
1 lemon, cut into wedges

1 For the dressing: Combine the mustard, vinegar, Worcestershire sauce, anchovies, garlic and lemon juice in a blender and blend well. With the motor running, pour in the olive oil in a slow steady stream until smooth. Add the parmesan, salt and pepper and blend again.

2 For the chicken: Carefully slice each chicken breast in half horizontally to make 6 thin pieces. Place each piece between 2 sheets of waxed paper and pound to an even thickness using the smooth side of a mallet or a rolling pin.

3 Whisk the milk, mustard and eggs in a shallow dish. Place the flour in another dish; season with salt and pepper. Mix the breadcrumbs and parmesan in a third dish. Set the 3 dishes aside. Season the chicken with salt and pepper on both sides. Dredge in the flour, then dip in the egg mixture and then coat in the breadcrumbs. Place on a plate until ready to cook.

4 Heat the olive oil in a large cast-iron skillet over medium-high heat. Add 2 or 3 pieces of chicken and cook until golden brown and cooked through, 2 to 3 minutes per side. Transfer to a rack set on a baking sheet and repeat with the remaining chicken, adding more oil as needed.

5 Toss the lettuce with the dressing. Top with more parmesan. Serve the chicken with the salad and lemon wedges.

STEP BY STEP

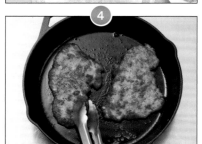

"I've used this salad dressing recipe for years—it makes me so happy!"

Pork

Grilled Pork Tenderloin with Broccolini

Prep time: 20 min ★ Total time: 40 min (plus marinating)
Serves: 4 to 6

¼	cup mirin
¼	cup low-sodium soy sauce
¼	cup rice vinegar
2	tablespoons packed light brown sugar
1	teaspoon toasted sesame oil
2	scallions, thinly sliced
¼	cup plus 1 tablespoon vegetable oil
3	garlic cloves, thinly sliced
1	3-inch piece fresh ginger, peeled and thinly sliced
2	pork tenderloins (about 2½ pounds total)
1½	pounds broccolini
1	teaspoon salt

White rice, for serving

1 Whisk the mirin, soy sauce, vinegar, brown sugar, sesame oil, scallions, ¼ cup vegetable oil and two-thirds of the garlic and ginger in a 9 x 13-inch baking dish. Add the pork and turn to coat. Cover and marinate in the refrigerator for at least 2 hours or overnight.

2 Heat a grill or grill pan to medium high. Remove the pork from the marinade, allowing the excess to drip off. Transfer the marinade to a small saucepan, bring to a boil over high heat and boil to reduce slightly, about 5 minutes. Set aside to cool.

3 Meanwhile, grill the pork, turning occasionally, until a meat thermometer inserted into the center reaches 145°, 20 to 30 minutes. Remove to a cutting board and let rest for 10 minutes.

4 Heat the remaining 1 tablespoon vegetable oil in a large skillet over medium-high heat. Add the remaining garlic and ginger and cook until fragrant, about 30 seconds. Add the broccolini along with ¾ cup water and the salt. Cover and steam until the broccolini is bright green and crisp-tender, 5 to 6 minutes.

5 Slice the pork and serve with the broccolini and rice. Drizzle the reduced marinade on top.

STEP BY STEP

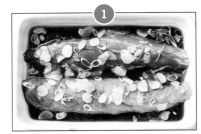

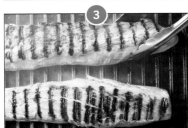

"Pork tenderloin is great for marinating—it soaks up tons of flavor."

"It's really satisfying to flatten the pork chops. Pound away your frustrations!"

Pork Milanese

Prep time: 40 min ★ Total time: 40 min ★ Serves: 6

6   boneless pork loin chops (about 5 ounces each)
¾   cup all-purpose flour
Kosher salt and black pepper, to taste
¼   cup half-and-half or whole milk
3   large eggs
1½   cups seasoned breadcrumbs
3 to 4 tablespoons olive oil
3 to 4 tablespoons salted butter
1   small piece parmesan cheese
5   ounces baby arugula, baby spinach or spring greens
2   lemons, cut into wedges

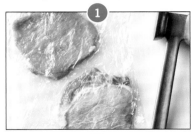

1. Place the pork chops between 2 sheets of plastic wrap and use a mallet or a rolling pin to pound them very thin (no thicker than ¼ inch). If you think they're thin enough, pound 'em a few more times—the thinner the better!

2. Place the flour in a shallow dish and mix in some salt and pepper. In another dish, whisk together the half-and-half and eggs. Place the breadcrumbs in a third dish. Set the 3 dishes aside.

3. Season both sides of the pork chops with salt and pepper. Coat them one at a time in the flour, then in the egg mixture and then in the breadcrumbs. Lay in a single layer on a baking sheet until you're ready to cook them.

4. Combine 1 tablespoon each olive oil and butter in a large cast-iron skillet over medium-low heat. When the butter is melted and hot, add 2 breaded pork chops and cook until the breading is golden brown and the pork is cooked through, about 2 minutes per side (add more oil or butter to the skillet when you flip, if necessary). Remove to a plate lined with paper towels. Repeat with the remaining oil, butter and pork in 2 more batches.

5. Shave the parmesan using a vegetable peeler. Place a piece of pork on each plate and top with the greens. Squeeze a little lemon juice over the greens, then sprinkle with a little salt. Top with the parmesan shavings and serve with more lemon wedges.

Slow-Cooker Teriyaki Ribs

Prep time: 15 min ★ Total time: 8 hr 15 min ★ Serves: 4 to 6

RIBS

2	racks baby back ribs (about 5 pounds total)
1	head garlic, cloves peeled and roughly chopped
1	3-inch piece fresh ginger, peeled and roughly chopped
½	cup honey
½	cup low-sodium soy sauce
½	cup rice vinegar
2	tablespoons cornstarch

SLAW

¼	cup mayonnaise
¼	cup rice vinegar
2	teaspoons honey
1	pound shredded coleslaw mix
1	small red onion, thinly sliced
1	cup fresh cilantro

Kosher salt and black pepper, to taste

❶ For the ribs: Cut each rack of ribs in half. Scatter the garlic and ginger in the bottom of a 6-quart slow cooker, then top with the ribs, bone-side down. Cover and cook on low heat for 8 hours, making sure not to lift the lid or otherwise disturb the ribs.

❷ Transfer the ribs to a baking sheet and loosely cover with foil to keep warm.

❸ Strain the cooking juices from the slow cooker into a large skillet. Stir in the honey, soy sauce and vinegar. Bring to a boil over medium-high heat. Stir the cornstarch with 2 tablespoons water in a small bowl, then whisk into the skillet and simmer until thickened, about 1 minute.

❹ Remove 3 tablespoons of the sauce to a small bowl and set aside for the slaw. Add the ribs to the remaining sauce in the skillet and turn to coat. Keep warm over low heat while you make the slaw.

❺ For the slaw: Whisk the mayonnaise, vinegar, honey and reserved sauce in a large bowl. Add the coleslaw mix, red onion and cilantro and toss to coat well. Season with salt and pepper if needed. Cut the ribs into pieces and serve with the slaw.

STEP BY STEP

"These baby backs are succulent and delicious!"

"I love, love, love a good sheet-pan dinner!"

Tuscan Pork Sheet-Pan Supper

Prep time: 35 min ★ Total time: 1 hr 30 min ★ Serves: 4 to 6

⅓   cup balsamic vinegar
5   garlic cloves, minced
⅓   cup plus ¼ cup olive oil, plus more for the pans
4   teaspoons dried oregano
2   teaspoons kosher salt, plus more to taste
1½ teaspoons black pepper
2   pork tenderloins (each slightly over 1 pound)
6   sweet potatoes, each cut into 6 wedges
6   shallots, quartered
Chopped fresh parsley, for topping

1. Whisk the balsamic vinegar, garlic, ⅓ cup olive oil, 2 teaspoons oregano and 1 teaspoon each salt and pepper in a small bowl.

2. Place the pork in a large resealable plastic bag and pour in the marinade. Seal the bag, place in a dish and marinate for 30 minutes at room temperature or 2 hours in the refrigerator.

3. Position racks in the upper and lower thirds of the oven and preheat to 450°. Toss the sweet potatoes and shallots with the remaining ¼ cup olive oil, 1 teaspoon salt, 2 teaspoons oregano and ½ teaspoon pepper in a large bowl.

4. Lightly oil 2 sheet pans. Put a pork tenderloin on each pan (let some of the marinade drip off first) and season lightly with salt. Arrange the sweet potatoes and shallots cut-sides down around each tenderloin.

5. Roast, rotating the pans halfway through and shaking them to loosen the potatoes, until a thermometer inserted into the thickest part of the meat registers 140° to 145° and the potatoes are tender, 20 to 30 minutes. (If the potatoes are not done, remove the pork to a cutting board and continue cooking the veggies another 5 minutes.) Slice the pork and serve with the vegetables. Top with parsley.

STEP BY STEP

Sausage and Rice Stuffed Peppers

Prep time: 30 min ★ Total time: 1 hr ★ Serves: 6

6	large red, orange and/or yellow bell peppers
3	tablespoons olive oil
1	pound loose sweet Italian sausage
4	plum tomatoes, diced
2	red onions, diced
3	garlic cloves, minced
1	teaspoon dried Italian seasoning

Kosher salt and black pepper, to taste

2	cups cooked brown rice (thawed if frozen)
2	cups shredded mozzarella cheese

1 Cut the tops off the peppers. Remove and discard the stems, then finely chop the tops; set aside. Scoop out the seeds and as much of the membranes as you can. Place the peppers in a microwave-safe bowl, add ½ cup water and cover with plastic wrap. Microwave until just beginning to soften, about 12 minutes, then uncover and set aside.

2 Preheat the oven to 450°. Heat 2 tablespoons olive oil in a large skillet over medium-high heat. Add the sausage and cook, breaking it up with a wooden spoon, until cooked through, about 6 minutes. Remove to a plate.

3 Add the remaining 1 tablespoon olive oil to the pan. Add the tomatoes, red onions, garlic, Italian seasoning and the chopped pepper tops and cook, stirring, until tender and lightly browned, 10 to 12 minutes.

4 Season the mixture with salt and pepper and stir in the sausage and rice. Taste and adjust the seasoning.

5 Place the peppers upright in a baking dish just large enough to hold them. Fill with the rice mixture and bake for 10 minutes. Sprinkle with the cheese and continue baking until the cheese is browned in spots, 10 to 12 more minutes.

STEP BY STEP

"*Assemble these ahead of time and refrigerate, then bake when it's time to eat!*"

"Noodles and salads are two of my favorite things to eat!"

Sesame Pork Noodle Salad

Prep time: 45 min ★ Total time: 50 min ★ Serves: 4 to 6

½ cup low-sodium soy sauce
2 tablespoons olive oil
2 tablespoons rice wine vinegar
4 teaspoons packed light brown sugar
1 tablespoon toasted sesame oil
2 teaspoons minced fresh ginger
2 garlic cloves, minced
Vegetable oil, for the grill
2 pork tenderloins (2 pounds total)
Kosher salt and black pepper, to taste
3 3-ounce packages ramen noodles
(seasoning packets discarded)
8 ounces snow peas, cut into thirds
1 7-ounce bag bean sprouts (3 cups)
3 cups shredded coleslaw mix
4 scallions, thinly sliced
1½ cups fresh cilantro
1 Fresno chile pepper, thinly sliced (optional)

STEP BY STEP

1 Make the dressing: Whisk the soy sauce, olive oil, vinegar, brown sugar, sesame oil, ginger and garlic in a medium bowl. Set aside.

2 Preheat a grill to medium high and oil the grates. Season the pork with salt and pepper on both sides and grill, turning occasionally, until a thermometer inserted into the center registers 145°, 17 to 22 minutes.

3 Remove the pork to a cutting board and let rest 10 minutes, then slice. Place in a large bowl, add ¼ cup of the dressing and toss to coat.

4 Meanwhile, bring a large pot of water to a boil. Add the ramen and cook according to the package directions, adding the snow peas during the last minute of cooking. Drain the noodles and snow peas and run under cool water.

5 Place the noodles and snow peas in a large bowl. Snip the noodles into smaller pieces with kitchen shears. Add the bean sprouts, coleslaw mix and remaining dressing and toss. Add the scallions, cilantro and chile (if using) and toss again. Add the pork and lightly toss, or serve the pork over the noodles.

White Pizza with Butternut Squash and Prosciutto

Prep time: 20 min ★ Total time: 1 hr ★ Serves: 4 to 6

1   small butternut squash, peeled, halved lengthwise, seeded and thinly sliced into half-moons
1   sprig rosemary
2   tablespoons olive oil
1½   teaspoons kosher salt
Black pepper, to taste
1½   pounds refrigerated pizza dough, at room temperature
2   cups shredded whole-milk mozzarella cheese
¼   cup grated pecorino cheese
1   cup whole-milk ricotta cheese
4   ounces thinly sliced prosciutto, torn into pieces

1 Preheat the oven to 500°. Combine the squash, rosemary, olive oil, 1 teaspoon salt and a few grinds of pepper on a rimmed baking sheet. Toss to coat, then spread the squash in a single layer. Roast until just tender but not completely cooked through (the squash will finish cooking on the pizza), about 10 minutes. Remove the squash to a plate; discard the rosemary.

2 Let the baking sheet cool for 5 minutes, then stretch the pizza dough on the pan with your fingers until it reaches the edges. Sprinkle with the mozzarella and pecorino.

3 Combine the ricotta with the remaining ½ teaspoon salt and a few grinds of pepper in a medium bowl.

4 Dollop the ricotta all over the pizza. Scatter the butternut squash on top of the cheese, making sure that some of the ricotta is showing through. Gather the prosciutto into clusters and scatter over the pizza.

5 Bake until the cheese is melted and starting to turn brown in spots and the dough is completely cooked through and golden brown around the edges, 20 to 25 minutes. Let cool for 5 minutes before slicing.

STEP BY STEP

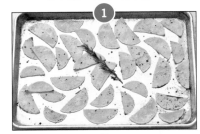

"The sweet and salty flavors in this pizza are in beautiful harmony!"

"This herb rub is a keeper— you can also use it on chicken or steak."

Italian Pork Sandwiches

Prep time: 30 min ★ Total time: 40 min ★ Serves: 6

4   teaspoons ground fennel
4   teaspoons dried rosemary
2   teaspoons dried oregano
2   teaspoons garlic salt
2   teaspoons kosher salt
Black pepper, to taste
2   1-pound pork tenderloins
5   tablespoons olive oil

2   garlic cloves
¼   teaspoon red pepper flakes
2   bunches broccolini, ends trimmed
½   cup mayonnaise
½   teaspoon grated lemon zest
6   ciabatta rolls, split and toasted
3   jarred roasted red bell peppers, sliced

1 Preheat the oven to 350˚. Combine the fennel, rosemary, oregano, garlic salt, 1 teaspoon salt and a generous amount of pepper in a small bowl.

2 Slice the pork tenderloins in half crosswise and rub evenly with the spice mixture.

3 Heat 3 tablespoons olive oil in a large cast-iron skillet over medium-high heat. Add the pork and sear, turning, until golden brown on all sides, about 5 minutes.

4 Place the skillet in the oven and bake until the pork is cooked through and a thermometer inserted into the middle registers 140˚, 18 to 20 minutes. Remove the pork to a cutting board and let rest for 5 minutes before thinly slicing.

5 Meanwhile, heat the remaining 2 tablespoons olive oil in a deep skillet over medium heat. Thinly slice 1 garlic clove and add it to the skillet along with the red pepper flakes; cook, stirring occasionally, until the garlic just starts to turn golden, 3 to 4 minutes. Add the broccolini and the remaining 1 teaspoon salt and toss. Cover the pan and cook, tossing a few times, until the broccolini is tender and bright green, 6 to 7 minutes.

6 Grate the remaining garlic clove and combine it with the mayonnaise and lemon zest in a small bowl. Generously spread the garlic mayonnaise on the rolls; top with a few slices each of pork and roasted red pepper. Serve the sandwiches with the broccolini.

STEP BY STEP

BLT Baked Potatoes

Prep time: 20 min ★ Total time: 1 hr 15 min ★ Serves: 6

6	medium russet potatoes
8	slices bacon
¼	cup buttermilk
¼	cup mayonnaise
2	teaspoons apple cider vinegar
¼	teaspoon garlic powder
3	scallions, chopped

1	tablespoon dijon mustard
1½	teaspoons black pepper
	Kosher salt, to taste
1	stick salted butter, at room temperature
1	romaine lettuce heart, shredded
1	pint cherry tomatoes, halved

1 Preheat the oven to 350°. Poke a few holes in the potatoes with a fork. Bake until the potatoes are tender and can easily be pierced with a fork, 50 to 60 minutes.

2 Meanwhile, cook the bacon in a large cast-iron skillet over medium-high heat, turning occasionally, until crisp, about 8 minutes. Drain on paper towels and crumble.

3 For the dressing: Whisk the buttermilk, mayonnaise, vinegar, garlic powder, one-third of the scallions, 1 teaspoon of the mustard, ½ teaspoon pepper and salt to taste in a medium bowl. Refrigerate until ready to serve.

4 Mash the butter with the remaining scallions, 2 teaspoons mustard and 1 teaspoon pepper in a small bowl with a fork.

5 Make a slit down the length of each potato. Using a kitchen towel, lightly squeeze the ends of each potato to open it up. Mash the insides of the potatoes slightly with a fork, then divide the scallion butter among them.

6 Toss the lettuce, bacon and tomatoes in a large bowl. Place each potato on a plate. Pile the salad on top and drizzle with the dressing.

STEP BY STEP

"Who doesn't love a BLT or a baked potato? This dish is the best of both worlds."

"Lettuce wraps are everything! It's fun to let people build their own."

Pork Bánh Mì Lettuce Wraps

Prep time: 30 min ★ Total time: 1 hr ★ Serves: 4 to 6

4	ounces thin rice noodles
3	radishes, thinly sliced
2	medium carrots, grated
2	tablespoons sugar
3	tablespoons rice vinegar
½	teaspoon kosher salt
½	cup mayonnaise
3	tablespoons Sriracha
⅓	cup hoisin sauce

⅓	cup soy sauce
2	tablespoons grated fresh ginger
3	garlic cloves, grated
1½	pounds boneless pork chops, cut into ½-inch pieces
3	tablespoons vegetable oil
2	heads butter lettuce (about 18 leaves)
¼	cup fresh cilantro, torn

1. Bring a medium pot of water to a boil. Add the noodles and cook until barely tender, about 4 minutes. Drain the noodles and submerge in a bowl of cold water to cool.

2. Combine the radishes and carrots with the sugar, 2 tablespoons rice vinegar and the salt in a medium bowl, making sure the vegetables are coated with the vinegar. Cover and refrigerate for at least 30 minutes and up to 2 hours.

3. Meanwhile, stir the mayonnaise, 1 tablespoon Sriracha and 2 teaspoons water in a small bowl. Cover and refrigerate until ready to serve.

4. Mix the hoisin sauce, soy sauce, ginger, garlic and the remaining 2 tablespoons Sriracha and 1 tablespoon rice vinegar in a large bowl. Add the pork and toss to coat. Cover and refrigerate for at least 30 minutes or overnight.

5. Heat 2 tablespoons vegetable oil in a large skillet over medium heat. Use a slotted spoon to remove the pork from the marinade and add it to the skillet. Cook, stirring, until cooked through, 4 to 5 minutes. Transfer to a bowl.

6. Drain the noodles and toss with the remaining 1 tablespoon vegetable oil. Drain the carrot mixture. To assemble, put some noodles in each lettuce leaf and top with pork, carrot mixture, Sriracha mayonnaise and cilantro.

STEP BY STEP

Sheet-Pan Ranch Pork and Veggies

Prep time: 20 min ★ Total time: 40 min ★ Serves: 4 to 6

5	tablespoons olive oil
2	tablespoons Worcestershire sauce
1	1-ounce packet ranch dressing mix
1	teaspoon black pepper
¼	teaspoon kosher salt
1	large yellow squash, sliced ½ inch thick
1	large zucchini, sliced ½ inch thick
2	large red bell peppers, cut into 1-inch-wide strips
1	red onion, cut into 1-inch wedges
8	boneless pork chops (½ inch thick; about 2 pounds total)
½	teaspoon paprika
¼	cup fresh parsley, finely chopped

1. Preheat the oven to 475°. Whisk the olive oil, Worcestershire sauce, ranch dressing mix, black pepper and salt in a large bowl until combined. Transfer 3 tablespoons to a small bowl and set aside for brushing.

2. Add the squash, zucchini, bell peppers and red onion to the large bowl with the marinade and toss until coated.
3. Spread out the vegetables in an even layer on a sheet pan. Bake until softened and golden brown in spots, about 30 minutes.

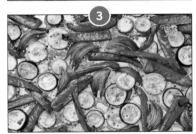

4. Meanwhile, place the pork chops on a second sheet pan and brush both sides with the reserved marinade. Sprinkle 1 side with the paprika. Toward the end of the vegetable roasting time, add the pork to the oven and cook until no longer pink in the middle, about 7 minutes. Sprinkle the pork and vegetables with the parsley.

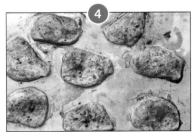

STEP BY STEP

"*A packet of ranch dressing mix gives this dinner so much flavor.*"

"These gnocchi get nice and crisp in the oven!"

Sheet-Pan Gnocchi with Spicy Sausage and Peppers

Prep time: 15 min ★ Total time: 55 min ★ Serves: 4 to 6

2   pounds hot Italian sausage
1½   pounds packaged gnocchi
4   bell peppers (any color), cut into ½-inch-thick strips
3   small red onions, thickly sliced
1   head garlic, cloves smashed and peeled
1½   teaspoons dried oregano
1   teaspoon kosher salt
6   tablespoons olive oil
½   cup grated pecorino cheese
¼   cup chopped fresh parsley
Balsamic glaze, for drizzling

1 Preheat the oven to 450°. Line 2 rimmed baking sheets with foil. Cut the sausage into 1-inch pieces.

2 Divide the sausage pieces, gnocchi, bell peppers, red onions and garlic between the 2 baking sheets. Sprinkle with the oregano and salt. Drizzle 3 tablespoons olive oil over each baking sheet and toss to coat the ingredients in the oil.

3 Bake, switching the baking sheets halfway through, until the vegetables are tender and caramelized, the sausage is cooked through and the gnocchi is crisp and golden, 35 to 40 minutes.

4 Sprinkle the pecorino and parsley over both baking sheets. Top each serving with a drizzle of balsamic glaze.

STEP BY STEP

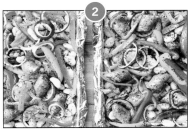

Breakfast-for-Dinner Sandwiches

Prep time: 40 min ★ Total time: 40 min ★ Serves: 6

POTATOES

2	pounds red new potatoes, cut into 1-inch chunks
1	large onion, chopped
3	tablespoons olive oil
1½	teaspoons sweet paprika
1	teaspoon kosher salt
½	teaspoon garlic powder

Black pepper, to taste

SANDWICHES

6	English muffins, split
6	slices fontina cheese
1	tablespoon salted butter
6	large eggs

Kosher salt and black pepper, to taste

12	slices tomatoes
2	ounces thinly sliced prosciutto
2	cups baby arugula
⅓	cup mayonnaise

1 For the potatoes: Place a baking sheet on the bottom oven rack and preheat to 450°. Combine the potatoes and onion in a large bowl. Drizzle with the olive oil and sprinkle with the paprika, salt, garlic powder and a generous amount of black pepper. Toss well.

2 Spread the potato mixture on the hot baking sheet and roast, tossing halfway through, until the potatoes are nicely browned and crispy, 20 to 25 minutes.

3 Meanwhile, for the sandwiches: Put the English muffins on a second baking sheet and bake on the top oven rack until lightly toasted, about 4 minutes. Remove the muffin tops and lay a piece of cheese on each of the muffin bottoms. Return to the oven to melt the cheese, 1 to 2 minutes.

4 Heat a large nonstick skillet over medium heat, add the butter and let melt. Crack the eggs into the skillet and season with salt and pepper. Cover the skillet and cook until the eggs are done to your liking, about 4 minutes for set whites with runny yolks.

5 To assemble, use a spatula or a round biscuit cutter to cut the eggs into 6 portions. Top each muffin bottom with 2 tomato slices, some prosciutto, an egg and some arugula. Spread the muffin tops with the mayonnaise and close the sandwiches. Serve with the potatoes.

STEP BY STEP

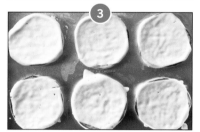

"This is inspired by my favorite breakfast sandwich at The Merc!"

"I love the combo of cool, crunchy vegetables with warm pork and noodles."

Rice Noodle Bowls with Soy-Sesame Pork

Prep time: 35 min ★ Total time: 55 min ★ Serves: 4 to 6

2	small pork tenderloins (about 2 pounds total), halved crosswise
½	cup low-sodium soy sauce
¼	cup fish sauce
2	tablespoons honey
1	tablespoon toasted sesame oil
2	tablespoons plus ⅓ cup rice vinegar
2	tablespoons sugar
2	teaspoons kosher salt, plus more to taste
2	teaspoons grated fresh ginger
4	radishes, thinly sliced
2	Persian cucumbers, thinly sliced into half-moons
1	large carrot, thinly sliced on an angle
½	small red onion, thinly sliced
12	ounces rice vermicelli
3	tablespoons vegetable oil

Sriracha mayonnaise and fresh cilantro and mint, for topping

1 Preheat the oven to 425°. Put the pork in a small baking dish. Combine the soy sauce, fish sauce, honey, sesame oil and 2 tablespoons of the rice vinegar in a liquid measuring cup. Pour all but ¼ cup of the mixture over the pork and let marinate at room temperature, turning occasionally, while you prepare the vegetables and noodles (up to 2 hours). Set the remaining marinade aside.

2 For the pickled vegetables: Combine the sugar, remaining ⅓ cup rice vinegar and the salt in a small saucepan. Bring to a simmer, then stir in the ginger. Put the radishes, cucumbers, carrot and red onion in a bowl. Pour in the vinegar mixture and add ½ cup ice, stirring to melt. Refrigerate until ready to serve.

3 Cook the rice noodles according to the package directions. Rinse under cold water and pat dry. Toss in a large bowl with the reserved ¼ cup marinade and 2 tablespoons vegetable oil. Season with salt and set aside.

4 Heat the remaining 1 tablespoon vegetable oil in a large skillet over medium-high heat. Add the pork and cook, turning, until browned on all sides, 3 to 4 minutes. Wipe out the baking dish. Return the pork to the dish and transfer to the oven. Bake until the internal temperature reaches 145°, 12 to 15 minutes. Let rest 5 minutes; slice.

5 Divide the noodles among serving bowls. Top with the pork and pickled vegetables and drizzle with a little of the pickling liquid. Top with Sriracha mayonnaise, cilantro and mint.

STEP BY STEP

Polenta with Sausage and Peppers

Prep time: 45 min ★ Total time: 45 min ★ Serves: 4 to 6

1	tablespoon olive oil
8	links sweet Italian sausage
3	assorted bell peppers, sliced
1	medium onion, sliced
3	cloves garlic, sliced
2	teaspoons kosher salt
1	cup low-sodium chicken broth

2	tablespoons balsamic vinegar
1½	cups polenta
Black pepper, to taste	
2	tablespoons salted butter, cut into pieces
½	cup grated parmesan cheese, plus more for topping
Sliced fresh basil, for topping	

1 Heat the olive oil in a large skillet over medium-high heat. Add the sausage and cook, turning, until browned on all sides, about 10 minutes. Remove the sausage to a plate.

2 Add the bell peppers and onion to the pan and cook, stirring, until the peppers are soft and the onion starts to caramelize, 8 to 10 minutes. Add the garlic and ½ teaspoon salt and cook for 1 minute.

3 Add the chicken broth and balsamic vinegar to the pan and stir. Add the sausage and any accumulated juices from the plate, nestling the sausage in the pepper and onion mixture. Bring to a simmer, then partially cover, reduce the heat to low and simmer until the sausage is cooked through, about 8 minutes.

4 Meanwhile, combine 4½ cups water and the remaining 1½ teaspoons salt in a saucepan. Bring to a simmer, then add the polenta and stir to combine. Reduce the heat to low and simmer, stirring, until thickened and the polenta is tender, about 5 minutes. Stir in the butter and parmesan and remove from the heat. Cover and let sit for 5 minutes.

5 Remove the sausage from the pan and slice, then return to the pan and toss. Remove from the heat.

6 Spoon the polenta onto plates. Top with the peppers, onion, sausage and any extra sauce from the pan. Top with more parmesan and basil.

STEP BY STEP

"Polenta is creamy and dreamy— and it's the easiest thing in the world to make!"

Beef

Hawaiian Pizza Burgers

Prep time: 20 min ★ Total time: 30 min ★ Serves: 6

3   pounds ground beef
1   tablespoon salt
1½   teaspoons black pepper
2   large Roma tomatoes
1   teaspoon olive oil, plus more for grilling
1   pineapple, peeled, cored and cut into rings
6   slices cheddar cheese

3   thick slices deli ham, halved crosswise
Butter, for the rolls
6   kaiser rolls or hamburger buns, split
½   red onion, very thinly sliced
Lettuce, for topping
Potato chips, for serving

1 Heat a grill or grill pan to medium high. Mix the ground beef in a large bowl with 2 teaspoons salt and the pepper. Form the mixture into 6 equal patties.

2 Halve the tomatoes lengthwise and toss with the olive oil and the remaining 1 teaspoon salt.

3 Brush the grill grates with olive oil. Place the tomatoes and pineapple slices on the grill and cook until softened and grill marks form, 5 to 6 minutes per side.

4 Meanwhile, grill the beef patties until marked, 4 to 5 minutes, then flip and cook 2 to 3 minutes longer.

5 Top each burger with a slice each of cheddar and ham and cook until the cheese melts, 2 to 3 minutes longer.

6 Butter the rolls and grill them until golden brown and marked, 1 to 2 minutes. Chop the grilled tomatoes and spread on both sides of each roll. Top with the burgers, a few red onion slices, some lettuce and grilled pineapple, then bring all the craziness together. Serve with chips.

STEP BY STEP

"This is a meat lover's dream!"

"Before you make this stir-fry, freeze the raw steak for a bit to make it easier to slice."

Hoisin Steak and Pepper Stir-Fry

Prep time: 30 min ★ Total time: 1 hr ★ Serves: 4 to 6

1¼   pounds boneless sirloin steak (¾ to 1 inch thick)
⅓   cup hoisin sauce
⅓   cup low-sodium soy sauce
2   tablespoons packed light brown sugar
1   tablespoon rice wine vinegar
2   tablespoons grated peeled fresh ginger
2   teaspoons Sriracha, plus more to taste
3   garlic cloves, grated
2   teaspoons cornstarch
4   tablespoons peanut or vegetable oil
3   red and/or yellow bell peppers, sliced ¼ inch thick
White rice, for serving
Sliced scallions and chopped fresh cilantro, for topping

1. Freeze the steak for 20 to 30 minutes to firm it up, then thinly slice against the grain and put in a large bowl.
2. Mix the hoisin sauce, soy sauce, brown sugar, vinegar, ginger, Sriracha, garlic and cornstarch in a separate bowl. Add ¼ cup of the sauce to the bowl with the steak and toss. Let marinate for 5 to 10 minutes.
3. Heat 1 tablespoon oil in a large skillet over medium-high heat. Add half of the bell peppers and cook, stirring, until blackened in spots, about 1 minute. Spread out on a baking sheet and repeat with another 1 tablespoon oil and the remaining peppers. Add to the baking sheet. (Spreading out the peppers prevents them from steaming.)
4. Add 1 tablespoon oil to the skillet. Add half of the steak in an even layer. Let cook about 20 seconds so that it starts to color, then toss and continue cooking just until the meat is no longer pink, another 30 seconds. Empty the steak onto a plate. Repeat with the remaining oil and steak.
5. Return the steak and peppers to the skillet and stir in the remaining sauce. Cook, tossing, until everything is well coated, about 1 minute. Serve over rice and top with scallions and cilantro.

STEP BY STEP

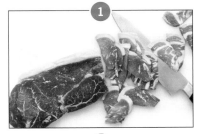

Spicy Steak with Pimiento Cheese Grits

Prep time: 40 min ★ Total time: 1 hr ★ Serves: 4 to 6

GRITS

1½	cups stone-ground grits
1	tablespoon kosher salt
1	cup half-and-half
4	ounces cream cheese, softened
2	cups grated cheddar cheese
2	4-ounce jars diced pimientos, drained
1	tablespoon dijon mustard

Black pepper, to taste

STEAK

1	tablespoon ground cumin
1	tablespoon chili powder
½	teaspoon garlic powder
3	1-inch-thick strip steaks (about 2 pounds)

Kosher salt

4	tablespoons salted butter, softened

1. For the grits: Bring 4 cups water to a boil in a medium saucepan. Whisk in the grits and salt. Reduce the heat to low, cover and cook, stirring occasionally, 30 minutes. Stir in the half-and-half and cook until the grits are tender and creamy, about 20 more minutes.

2. Add the cream cheese, cheddar cheese, pimientos and mustard and stir until everything is melted together. Season with pepper and remove from the heat.

3. Meanwhile, for the steak: Combine the cumin, chili powder and garlic powder in a small bowl. Heat a grill pan over medium-high heat. Pat the meat dry and season well with salt and the spice mix.

4. Brush the butter on the grill pan and grill the meat until well marked, 4 to 5 minutes per side, depending on how you like your beef cooked. Cover and set aside to rest before slicing, about 15 minutes.

5. Slice the steak and serve with the grits.

STEP BY STEP

"Grits are even better when they're extra cheesy!"

"Everything bagel seasoning is yummy on burger buns—it brings even more flavor to the scenario."

Everything Burgers

Prep time: 30 min ★ Total time: 30 min ★ Serves: 6

BUNS

2	teaspoons poppy seeds
2	teaspoons sesame seeds
1	teaspoon dried garlic flakes
1	teaspoon dried onion flakes
1	teaspoon kosher salt
1	large egg white
6	brioche buns

BURGERS

6	ounces cream cheese, at room temperature
3	tablespoons sun-dried tomato pesto
2	pounds ground beef
1	teaspoon kosher salt, plus more to taste

Black pepper, to taste
Shredded iceberg lettuce, sliced tomato
    and sliced red onion, for topping
Potato chips, for serving

1 For the buns: Preheat the oven to 375˚. Stir together the poppy seeds, sesame seeds, garlic flakes, onion flakes and salt in a small bowl. Whisk the egg white in another small bowl until foamy. Arrange the buns on a baking sheet. Brush the tops with the beaten egg white. Sprinkle with the everything seasoning. Bake until the seasoning is set, 5 to 6 minutes.

2 For the burgers: Preheat a grill or grill pan to medium high. Mix the cream cheese and sun-dried tomato pesto in a small bowl and set aside.

3 Break up the ground beef in a large bowl; season with the salt and pepper. Form into six ½-inch-thick patties; season lightly with more salt and pepper.

4 Grill the burgers until done to your liking, about 4 minutes per side for medium rare. Remove to a plate.

5 To serve, split the buns and spread a good amount of the cream cheese mixture on the insides. Place the burgers on the buns with the lettuce, tomato and red onion. Serve with potato chips.

STEP BY STEP

Steakhouse Kebabs

Prep time: 35 min ★ Total time: 1 hr ★ Serves: 4 to 6

BLUE CHEESE DRESSING

½   cup mayonnaise
¼   cup buttermilk
¼   cup sour cream
2   teaspoons apple cider vinegar
Dash of Worcestershire sauce
⅓   cup crumbled blue cheese
2   tablespoons chopped fresh parsley
Kosher salt and black pepper, to taste

KEBABS

1   pound small red potatoes, halved
Kosher salt
1   10-ounce package cremini mushrooms, trimmed,
    halved if large
¼   cup olive oil
½   teaspoon garlic powder
Black pepper, to taste
1¾   pounds boneless sirloin steak, cut into 1½-inch chunks
2   tablespoons Worcestershire sauce
Torn romaine lettuce, for serving

① For the blue cheese dressing: Stir together the mayonnaise, buttermilk, sour cream, vinegar and Worcestershire sauce in a medium bowl. Stir in the blue cheese and parsley and season with salt and pepper. Cover and refrigerate while you make the kebabs.

② For the kebabs: Soak 8 to 12 wooden skewers in water for 30 minutes. Preheat a grill or grill pan to medium. Put the potatoes in a saucepan with salted water to cover by 1 inch. Bring to a simmer and cook until a knife inserted into a potato slips out with just a little resistance, 8 to 10 minutes. Drain and pat dry.

③ Put the potatoes in a large bowl and add the mushrooms. Toss with 2 tablespoons olive oil, the garlic powder, ½ teaspoon salt and a generous amount of pepper.

④ Toss the steak in another bowl with the remaining 2 tablespoons olive oil, the Worcestershire sauce, ½ teaspoon salt and a generous amount of pepper. Thread the beef, mushrooms and potatoes onto the skewers.

⑤ Grill the kebabs, turning, until the vegetables are tender and the beef is charred, about 10 minutes. Let rest 5 minutes. Serve the kebabs with romaine and drizzle with some of the dressing. Serve with the remaining dressing.

STEP BY STEP

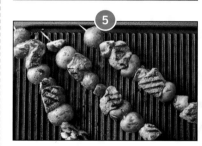

"Ladd loves to grill outside, but I'm more of a grill pan person!"

"*The slow cooker makes the meat insanely tender!*"

Slow-Cooker
Drip Beef Sandwiches

Prep time: 30 min ★ Total time: 7 hr 20 min ★ Serves: 6

1   2½-pound piece beef chuck roast
1   teaspoon minced fresh rosemary
¾   teaspoon kosher salt
Black pepper, to taste
1   12-ounce jar pepperoncini
1   cup beef broth
6   tablespoons salted butter, softened
1   large onion, sliced
6   soft hoagie rolls, split
12   slices provolone cheese
Potato chips, for serving

1 Toss the beef roast in a 6- to 8-quart slow cooker with the rosemary, ½ teaspoon salt and a generous grinding of pepper. Add the pepperoncini with their brine, along with the beef broth. Cover and cook on low until the meat is very tender and easy to pull apart, 7 to 8 hours.

2 When the slow cooker has about 15 minutes left, heat 2 tablespoons butter in a large skillet over medium-high heat. Add the onion, the remaining ¼ teaspoon salt and a few grinds of pepper. Cook, stirring occasionally, until tender and lightly browned, about 10 minutes.

3 Remove the roast to a bowl and shred using 2 forks, then return it to the slow cooker. Keep warm.

4 Preheat the broiler. Put the rolls on a baking sheet and spread with the remaining 4 tablespoons butter. Broil until toasted, about 2 minutes.

5 Heap a generous portion of meat on each roll, then spoon some of the cooking liquid over the meat. Top with a few pepperoncini from the slow cooker and plenty of caramelized onions. Put 2 slices of cheese on each sandwich and return to the broiler just to melt the cheese, about 1 more minute. Serve with potato chips and the extra cooking liquid on the side for dipping.

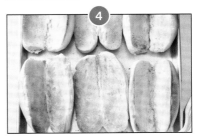

Steak Sandwiches with Wasabi Cream Sauce

Prep time: 30 min ★ Total time: 2 hr 30 min ★ Serves: 6

SAUCE

⅓   cup sour cream
¼   cup mayonnaise
1   tablespoon chopped fresh cilantro
1 to 2 teaspoons prepared wasabi paste
1   garlic clove, grated
¼   teaspoon kosher salt, plus more to taste
Black pepper, to taste

STEAK

2   pounds sirloin steak (about 1 inch thick)
Olive oil, for drizzling
1   teaspoon kosher salt
Black pepper, to taste
6   ciabatta rolls, split open
6   ounces sliced havarti or Swiss cheese
3   cups baby arugula
Potato chips, for serving

1 For the sauce: Combine the sour cream, mayonnaise, cilantro, wasabi, garlic, salt and a few grinds of pepper in a small bowl. Cover and refrigerate 2 hours.

2 For the steak: Preheat the oven to 425°. Heat a large cast-iron skillet over medium-high heat until hot. Drizzle the steak with olive oil and sprinkle with the salt and a few grinds of pepper. Add to the skillet and cook until browned, about 2 minutes per side.

3 Transfer the skillet to the oven and cook 5 to 7 minutes for medium rare. Remove steak to a cutting board and let rest.

4 Meanwhile, place the bottom halves of the rolls on a baking sheet and top with the cheese. Bake until the cheese starts to melt, about 3 minutes.

5 Slice the steak and place on the roll bottoms. Top with the arugula. Spread most of the wasabi sauce on the top halves of the rolls and close the sandwiches. Serve with potato chips and the remaining wasabi sauce for dipping—it goes great with the potato chips!

STEP BY STEP

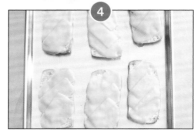

"Wasabi isn't just for sushi: It adds a nice horseradishy kick to every bite of these sandwiches."

"Use your leftover peanut sauce as a dip for veggies or drizzle it on a salad."

Grilled Steak Wraps with Peanut Sauce

Prep time: 45 min ★ Total time: 45 min ★ Serves: 4 to 6

PEANUT SAUCE
½ cup creamy peanut butter
½ cup canned coconut milk
¼ cup fresh lime juice
1 teaspoon fish sauce
½ teaspoon chili oil
2 garlic cloves, grated
1 1-inch piece fresh ginger, grated

SALAD
¼ cup fresh lime juice
1 tablespoon olive oil
1 teaspoon sugar
1 teaspoon fish sauce
1 teaspoon chili oil (optional)
4 radishes, cut into thin sticks
1 cup shredded carrots
2 romaine lettuce hearts, shredded
2 scallions, thinly sliced
½ cup fresh cilantro

WRAPS
2 skirt steaks (about 2¼ pounds total), each cut crosswise into 3 pieces
Kosher salt and black pepper, to taste
12 8-inch whole-wheat tortillas

1 Preheat a grill or grill pan to medium high. For the peanut sauce: Combine the peanut butter, coconut milk, lime juice, fish sauce, chili oil, garlic and ginger in a blender and puree until smooth. Pour into a medium bowl and set aside for topping.

2 For the salad: Whisk the lime juice, olive oil, sugar, fish sauce and chili oil (if using) in a large bowl.

3 Add the radishes, carrots, lettuce, scallions and cilantro to the dressing and toss to combine.

4 For the wraps: Season the steak with salt and pepper. Grill 5 to 6 minutes per side for medium doneness. Remove to a cutting board and let rest for 10 minutes.

5 Grill the tortillas until marked, about 2 minutes per side.

6 Slice the steak against the grain. Serve the steak and salad in the tortillas. Drizzle with the peanut sauce.

STEP BY STEP

Instant Pot BBQ Beef Sandwiches

Prep time: 25 min ★ Total time: 1 hr 30 min ★ Serves: 4 to 6

1	tablespoon chili powder
1	teaspoon ground cumin
1	teaspoon smoked paprika
1	teaspoon kosher salt, plus more to taste
¼	teaspoon cayenne pepper

Black pepper, to taste

1	2½- to 3-pound piece boneless beef chuck roast, trimmed and cut into 5 or 6 pieces
1	tablespoon vegetable oil
½	cup ketchup
½	cup apple cider vinegar
2	tablespoons molasses
2	tablespoons packed light brown sugar

Hot sauce, to taste

6	sesame hamburger buns, split and toasted

Coleslaw and pickles, for topping

Potato chips, for serving

① Whisk the chili powder, cumin, paprika, 1 teaspoon salt, the cayenne and a few grinds of black pepper in a large bowl. Add the beef and toss to coat well.

② Set a 6-quart Instant Pot to sauté on high. When hot, add the vegetable oil, then add the beef in a single layer and cook, turning, until browned, about 10 minutes. Remove the beef to a large plate and cancel the sauté setting.

③ Add ⅔ cup water to the pot. Use a wooden spoon to scrape up the bottom of the pot. Return the meat to the pot along with any juices from the plate. Put on and lock the lid, making sure the steam valve is in the sealing position. Set the pot to pressure-cook on high for 45 minutes. When the time is up, let the pressure release naturally for 15 minutes, then carefully turn the steam valve to the venting position to manually release any remaining pressure.

④ Meanwhile, stir the ketchup, vinegar, molasses and brown sugar in a small bowl. Add salt, pepper and hot sauce to taste. Remove the beef to a clean plate. Set the pot to sauté on high. Add the ketchup mixture and simmer until reduced by half, 15 to 20 minutes.

⑤ Meanwhile, shred the beef with 2 forks, discarding any large pieces of fat. Return to the pot and stir until well coated. Cancel the sauté setting and adjust the seasoning with salt, pepper and hot sauce. Divide the meat among the buns and top with coleslaw and pickles. Serve with chips.

"Give me shredded meat and a roll and I'm a happy camper."

"This saucy stir-fry is great over noodles or rice."

Beef and Broccoli Stir-Fry

Prep time: 45 min ★ Total time: 45 min ★ Serves: 4 to 6

Kosher salt, to taste
12 ounces spaghetti or angel hair pasta
3 tablespoons toasted sesame oil
⅓ cup low-sodium soy sauce
2 tablespoons sugar
2 tablespoons rice vinegar
4 garlic cloves, minced
1¼ pounds sirloin steak (about ¾ inch thick), thinly sliced against the grain

1 teaspoon cornstarch
4 tablespoons vegetable oil
1 head broccoli, cut into small florets (peel and thinly slice the stalks, too)
1 8-ounce can sliced water chestnuts
1 red Fresno chile pepper, halved and thinly sliced
3 scallions, thinly sliced

1 Bring a large pot of salted water to a boil. Add the pasta and cook as the label directs. Drain, transfer to a bowl and toss with 1 tablespoon sesame oil.

2 Mix the soy sauce, sugar, vinegar, garlic, the remaining 2 tablespoons sesame oil and ¼ cup water in a small bowl. Toss 3 tablespoons of the mixture with the beef in a medium bowl. Whisk the cornstarch into the remaining soy sauce mixture.

3 Heat 2 tablespoons vegetable oil in a large skillet over medium-high heat. Add the broccoli and let brown on the bottom, 1½ minutes, then toss and continue cooking, tossing occasionally, until bright green, 3 to 5 minutes. Season lightly with salt. Remove to a baking sheet.

4 Add another 1 tablespoon vegetable oil to the skillet and heat until shimmering. Add half the meat and let brown on the bottom, 30 seconds, then turn the meat and cook until the other side browns a bit, another 30 seconds. Add to the baking sheet with the broccoli. Repeat with the remaining 1 tablespoon vegetable oil and meat.

5 Reduce the heat to medium. Add the water chestnuts and half the chile to the skillet and toss just to heat, 30 seconds. Stir the soy sauce–cornstarch mixture, add it to the skillet and bring it to a simmer.

6 Add the broccoli and meat with any accumulated juices to the skillet and toss to coat and heat through, about 1 minute. Serve over the pasta and top with the scallions and remaining chile.

STEP BY STEP

Beef Curry with Sweet Potato Noodles

Prep time: 30 min ★ Total time: 30 min ★ Serves: 4 to 6

1	pound sweet potato noodles
3	tablespoons vegetable oil
1	pound sirloin steak (¾ inch thick), thinly sliced against the grain
3	teaspoons kosher salt

Black pepper, to taste

1	small head cauliflower, cut into small florets
1	onion, diced
1	tablespoon minced fresh ginger
1	garlic clove, minced
3	tablespoons red curry paste
1	13.5-ounce can coconut milk

Juice of ½ lime, plus wedges for serving

3	cups chopped curly kale
1	tablespoon torn fresh basil

1 Bring a few cups of water to a boil in a large pot with a steamer basket in place. Add the sweet potato noodles to the steamer, cover and cook until tender, about 5 minutes. Remove the steamer basket to the sink and let the noodles drain and dry out a little.

2 Meanwhile, heat 2 tablespoons vegetable oil in a large skillet over medium-high heat. Season the beef with 1 teaspoon salt and a few grinds of pepper. Add half of the beef to the skillet in a single layer and cook, undisturbed, until browned on the bottom, about 30 seconds. Flip the beef and cook just until the other side browns a bit, another 30 seconds. (It's OK if the beef is still pink in spots.) Transfer to a rimmed baking sheet and repeat with the remaining beef.

3 Heat the remaining 1 tablespoon oil in the skillet over medium-high heat. Add the cauliflower, onion, 1 teaspoon salt and a few grinds of pepper. Cook, undisturbed, until browned, 1 to 2 minutes. Stir, then continue to cook, stirring occasionally, until the onion starts softening, 2 to 3 minutes.

4 Add the ginger and garlic to the skillet and cook, stirring, until fragrant, 1 minute. Stir in the curry paste, then stir in the coconut milk and lime juice. Bring to a boil, then reduce the heat to medium and cook, stirring occasionally, until the cauliflower is tender, 5 to 6 minutes.

5 Stir in the kale, basil and the remaining 1 teaspoon salt and cook, stirring, until the kale is wilted, 1 minute. Stir in the beef. Serve over the sweet potato noodles with lime wedges.

STEP BY STEP

"I'm loving veggie noodles these days! You can buy them fresh or frozen."

"Zucchini boats are perfect for a hearty low-carb meal."

Chili-Stuffed Zucchini Boats

Prep time: 25 min ★ Total time: 1 hr 15 min ★ Serves: 6

6	medium zucchini
2	tablespoons olive oil, plus more for brushing
1	teaspoon kosher salt

Black pepper, to taste

1¾	pounds ground beef
1	small onion, chopped
½ to 1	poblano chile pepper, seeded and chopped
2	tablespoons chili powder
1	teaspoon ground cumin
¼	teaspoon cayenne pepper
¼	teaspoon garlic powder
2	tablespoons tomato paste
1	8-ounce can tomato sauce
¼	cup chopped fresh cilantro, plus more for garnish
1½	cups grated cheddar cheese

Sour cream and sliced scallions, for garnish

1 Preheat the oven to 400°. Cut the ends off the zucchini, then slice in half lengthwise. Use a spoon to scoop out the seeds and hollow out the centers. Brush with olive oil and season with ½ teaspoon salt and a few grinds of pepper. Set on a rimmed baking sheet.

2 Heat the olive oil in a large skillet over medium heat. Add the beef and cook, stirring and breaking up the meat, until browned, about 3 minutes.

3 Add the onion, poblano, chili powder, cumin, cayenne, garlic powder and the remaining ½ teaspoon salt and cook, stirring occasionally, until the vegetables begin to soften, about 4 minutes.

4 Add the tomato paste to the skillet and cook until darkened, about 1 minute. Stir in the tomato sauce and ¾ cup water until everything is combined. Reduce the heat to low and simmer until very thick, about 8 minutes. Stir in the cilantro. Let cool slightly.

5 Fill the zucchini boats with the chili and sprinkle with the cheese.

6 Cover with foil and bake until the zucchini is just tender, 18 to 20 minutes. Uncover and bake until the cheese is golden, 10 to 15 more minutes. Top with sour cream, scallions and cilantro.

STEP BY STEP

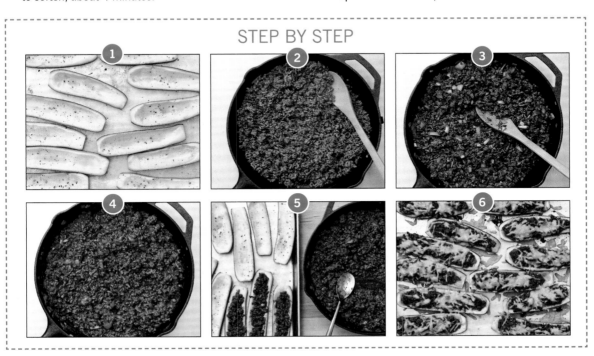

Instant Pot Pot Roast

Prep time: 20 min ★ Total time: 2 hr ★ Serves: 6 to 8

1   3- to 3½-pound beef chuck roast
Kosher salt and black pepper, to taste
2   tablespoons olive oil
2   large yellow onions, quartered
6   carrots, scrubbed and cut into large pieces
1   cup dry red wine
2   cups beef broth
3   sprigs fresh rosemary
3   sprigs fresh thyme
Mashed potatoes, for serving

❶ Set an Instant Pot to sauté and allow to heat up. Season the roast generously with salt and pepper. When the Instant Pot says "hot," add the olive oil. Add the meat and sear, turning, until browned on all sides, about 4 minutes. Remove to a clean plate.

❷ Add the onions and carrots to the Instant Pot and cook, stirring occasionally until lightly browned, 3 to 4 minutes.

❸ Deglaze the pot with the red wine, scraping the bottom of the pot to get all of the delicious bits. Add the broth, rosemary, thyme and the beef.

❹ Lock the lid into place, making sure the steam valve is in the sealing position. Push "manual" and set the pot to pressure-cook for 1 hour 20 minutes. The pot will release some steam as it comes up to pressure, then it will seal automatically. When the cooking time is done, let the Instant Pot naturally vent for at least 10 minutes—20 is better. Using a wooden spoon, carefully push the valve open to release the rest of the pressure. Remove the lid.

❺ Skim as much fat off the top of the liquid as you can before disturbing the roast. Remove the roast to a cutting board and shred with 2 forks. Serve with mashed potatoes, plus the carrots and onions. Top with the juices from the Instant Pot.

STEP BY STEP

"This roast tastes just like the classic— but it cooks in half the time!"

"These meatballs are also great as an appetizer—just serve them on toothpicks."

Ginger Meatballs with Sesame Broccoli

Prep time: 45 min ★ Total time: 45 min ★ Serves: 4 to 6

1½ pounds ground beef
1 large egg
½ onion, finely diced
¾ cup panko breadcrumbs
1½ teaspoons kosher salt
1 teaspoon black pepper
½ teaspoon red pepper flakes, plus more to taste
1 2-inch piece fresh ginger, peeled and grated
3 to 4 cups broccoli florets
¼ cup plus 1 tablespoon canola oil
1 tablespoon sesame seeds

2 teaspoons toasted sesame oil
2 cups beef broth
¼ cup hoisin sauce
¼ cup white wine vinegar or sherry vinegar
2 tablespoons low-sodium soy sauce
1 tablespoon cornstarch
⅓ cup all-purpose flour
1 red bell pepper, cut into strips
3 scallions, thinly sliced (white and green parts separated)
Cooked white rice, for serving

1 Preheat the oven to 425°. Combine the beef, egg, onion, panko, 1 teaspoon salt, ½ teaspoon black pepper, the red pepper flakes and half of the ginger in a large bowl and mix with your hands. Roll into 1-inch balls and place on a rimmed baking sheet; refrigerate while you make the broccoli.

2 Toss the broccoli with 1 tablespoon canola oil, the sesame seeds and the remaining ½ teaspoon each salt and pepper on a separate baking sheet. Roast, tossing once, until tender and starting to char, 10 to 15 minutes. Drizzle with the sesame oil.

3 Whisk the beef broth, hoisin sauce, vinegar, soy sauce and cornstarch in a bowl.

4 Toss the meatballs in the flour in a large bowl. Heat the remaining ¼ cup canola oil in a large cast-iron skillet over medium-high heat. Working in batches, add the meatballs and cook, turning, until browned, 2 to 3 minutes. Transfer to a plate.

5 Pour off the excess oil from the pan and return to medium-high heat. Add the bell pepper, scallion whites and remaining ginger and stir, 1 minute.

6 Add the broth mixture and meatballs to the skillet and stir. Cook, stirring, until the sauce has thickened and the meatballs are cooked through, about 3 minutes. Add more red pepper flakes to taste. Serve the meatball mixture and broccoli over rice and top with the scallion greens.

STEP BY STEP

Peppercorn-Crusted Steak with Creamed Spinach

Prep time: 40 min ★ Total time: 50 min ★ Serves: 4 to 6

1   **stick salted butter**
½   **onion, finely chopped**
4   **garlic cloves (2 finely chopped, 2 crushed)**
2   **12-ounce bags baby spinach**
4   **ounces cream cheese, cut into pieces**
1¼   **teaspoons kosher salt**
Black pepper, to taste
Pinch of ground nutmeg
¼   **cup tricolor peppercorns**
1   **teaspoon sugar**
1   **tri-tip or sirloin steak (1¾ to 2 pounds), at room temperature**
2   **tablespoons olive oil**
2   **large rosemary sprigs**

1. Melt 4 tablespoons butter in a large skillet over medium heat. Add the onion and cook, stirring occasionally, until soft but not browned, about 5 minutes. Add the chopped garlic and cook 30 seconds.

2. Add the spinach to the skillet in handfuls, stirring after each addition. Cook until all the spinach is wilted, about 12 minutes. Push the spinach to one side of the skillet. Add the cream cheese to the other side and smash it until mostly melted, about 2 minutes, then stir into the spinach. Stir in ¼ teaspoon salt, a few grinds of pepper and the nutmeg. Keep warm.

3. Put the peppercorns and sugar in a resealable plastic bag and crush using a rolling pin or skillet. Season the steak with the remaining 1 teaspoon salt, then coat both sides with the peppercorn mixture, pressing to adhere.

4. Heat a large cast-iron skillet over high heat. Swirl the olive oil in the pan. Add the steak and cook until well browned and the internal temperature registers between 105° and 110° on an instant-read thermometer, about 6 minutes per side.

5. Add the remaining 4 tablespoons butter, the rosemary and the crushed garlic to the skillet. Tilt the pan toward you and spoon the butter over the steak until the crust is burnished and the internal temperature is 115° for medium rare, about 5 more minutes.

6. Transfer the steak to a cutting board, cover with foil and let rest 10 minutes. Thinly slice the steak against the grain and serve with the creamed spinach.

STEP BY STEP

"Close your eyes and you'll think you're at a fancy steakhouse!"

"Caesar salad is a favorite of mine, and I love it even more with steak on top!"

Kale Caesar Salad with Steak

Prep time: 30 min ★ Total time: 1 hr ★ Serves: 4 to 6

CROUTONS

½	loaf crusty French bread, cut into 1-inch cubes (about 6 cups)
¼	cup olive oil
¼	teaspoon garlic powder
¼	teaspoon kosher salt

DRESSING

2	tablespoons dijon mustard
1	tablespoon red wine vinegar
1	teaspoon Worcestershire sauce
4	anchovy fillets
2	garlic cloves

Juice of ½ lemon

½	cup olive oil
¼	cup grated parmesan cheese

Kosher salt and black pepper, to taste

SALAD

2	pounds rib-eye, strip or sirloin steaks (about 1 inch thick)

Kosher salt and black pepper, to taste

1	tablespoon olive oil
1	bunch curly kale, leaves chopped
1	3-ounce piece parmesan cheese, shaved with a vegetable peeler

1 For the croutons: Preheat the oven to 250˚. Spread the bread cubes on a baking sheet, drizzle with the olive oil and toss. Sprinkle with the garlic powder and salt. Bake, shaking the pan occasionally, until the croutons are golden and crisp, 45 minutes to 1 hour. Let cool.

2 For the dressing: Combine the mustard, vinegar, Worcestershire sauce, anchovies, garlic and lemon juice in a blender or food processor. Pulse on low speed several times, then scrape down the sides and pulse again until fairly smooth. With the motor running, slowly drizzle in the olive oil. Scrape down the sides, add the parmesan and pulse. Add salt and pepper to taste.

3 For the salad: Season the steaks on both sides with salt and pepper. Heat the olive oil in a large cast-iron skillet over medium-high heat. Add the steaks and cook 2½ to 3 minutes per side for medium rare. Let rest 5 minutes.

4 Put the kale in a large bowl and add most of the shaved parmesan. Drizzle with half of the dressing and toss. Add the croutons and toss again. Add more dressing, if needed. Thinly slice the steak and add to the bowl. Top with the remaining shaved parmesan.

Instant Pot Ancho Beef Chili with Sweet Potatoes

Prep time: 35 min ★ Total time: 1 hr 15 min ★ Serves: 4 to 6

3	tablespoons ancho chile powder
2	teaspoons smoked paprika
1	teaspoon ground cumin
1	teaspoon dried oregano
1	teaspoon kosher salt, plus more to taste
½	teaspoon garlic powder
2	pounds boneless beef chuck, cut into 1-inch pieces
2	tablespoons olive oil
2	slices thick-cut bacon, chopped
2	medium onions, chopped
1	jalapeño pepper, finely chopped
1	14.5-ounce can diced fire-roasted tomatoes
1	cup low-sodium beef broth
1	pound sweet potatoes, peeled and cut into 1-inch chunks
2	tablespoons masa harina
1	tablespoon apple cider vinegar

Sour cream, grated Monterey Jack cheese and sliced scallions, for topping

1 Combine the chile powder, paprika, cumin, oregano, salt and garlic powder in a large bowl. Add the beef and toss.

2 Set a 6-quart Instant Pot to sauté on high. Add the olive oil, then the bacon and cook, stirring, until crisp, about 3 minutes. Remove to a paper towel–lined plate.

3 Add half of the beef to the Instant Pot. Cook, stirring, until browned, about 3 minutes. Remove to a plate and repeat with the remaining beef.

4 Add the onions and jalapeño to the pot and cook, stirring, until softened, 2 to 3 minutes. Add the tomatoes and broth and bring to a simmer. Return the beef to the pot along with the bacon and sweet potatoes. Stir to combine. Lock the lid in place, making sure the steam vent is in the sealing position. Set to pressure-cook on high for 25 minutes. When the time is up, let the pressure release naturally for 15 minutes. Remove the lid and switch back to the sauté setting on high to bring the liquid to boil.

5 Ladle 1 cup of the broth into a liquid measuring cup and whisk in the masa harina until smooth. Whisk the mixture into the chili, taking care not to break up the sweet potatoes too much. Simmer until thickened, 1 to 2 minutes. Stir in the vinegar and season with salt, if needed. Ladle the chili into bowls and top with sour cream, cheese and scallions.

"You can't watch football without a big pot of chili!"

Fish & Seafood

Sheet-Pan Salmon Puttanesca

Prep time: 15 min ★ Total time: 40 min ★ Serves: 6

3   cups sourdough bread cubes (1-inch pieces)
½   cup pitted niçoise olives
1   red onion, cut into wedges
1   pint cherry tomatoes
1   teaspoon kosher salt
Black pepper, to taste
¼   cup olive oil
6   6-ounce skinless salmon fillets
2   tablespoons red wine vinegar
1   tablespoon capers, drained
⅓   cup fresh parsley leaves, plus chopped parsley for topping

1 Preheat the oven to 375˚. Combine the bread cubes, olives, red onion and cherry tomatoes on a baking sheet. Sprinkle with ½ teaspoon salt and a few grinds of pepper and drizzle with 2 tablespoons olive oil. Toss until everything is evenly coated. Bake until the bread just starts to crisp, 12 to 15 minutes.

2 Rub the salmon with 1 tablespoon olive oil and sprinkle with ½ teaspoon salt. Arrange on the baking sheet among the bread mixture. Bake until the salmon is opaque and flakes easily with a fork, 8 to 12 minutes.

3 Meanwhile, whisk the remaining 1 tablespoon olive oil with the vinegar in a large bowl. Add the capers.

4 Arrange the salmon on a platter and top with chopped parsley. Add the bread mixture to the vinaigrette along with the parsley leaves. Toss until completely coated. Serve the salmon with the bread salad.

"This is a great way to cook salmon—and there's just one pan to clean up."

"Broiled shrimp is the best—it gets a little charred."

Ginger Shrimp Salad

Prep time: 25 min ★ Total time: 25 min ★ Serves: 4 to 6

SHRIMP

2 tablespoons soy sauce
2 tablespoons packed brown sugar
1 tablespoon minced fresh ginger
2 garlic cloves, minced
2 pounds large shrimp, peeled and deveined

DRESSING AND SALAD

¼ cup olive oil
¼ cup fresh lime juice (from 2 limes)
2 tablespoons packed brown sugar
1 tablespoon minced fresh ginger
½ jalapeño pepper, seeded and diced
1 pound mixed salad greens
1 pint cherry tomatoes, halved

1 For the shrimp: Mix the soy sauce, brown sugar, ginger and garlic in a large resealable plastic bag. Add the shrimp to the bag and seal. Let marinate at least 5 minutes and up to 15 minutes.

2 For the dressing: Whisk the olive oil, lime juice, brown sugar, ginger and jalapeño in a small bowl.

3 Preheat the broiler. Remove the shrimp from the marinade, transfer to a rimmed baking sheet or broiler pan and broil until opaque, pink and slightly charred, about 4 minutes. Transfer the shrimp to a plate and let cool slightly, saving any juices on the baking sheet.

4 For the salad: In a large bowl, toss the salad greens and tomatoes with about three-quarters of the dressing. Arrange the shrimp on top and drizzle with the remaining dressing and any juices from the baking sheet.

STEP BY STEP

Coconut Curry Shrimp with Potatoes and Kale

Prep time: 35 min ★ Total time: 1 hr ★ Serves: 4 to 6

½ cup coconut milk
2 tablespoons honey
Juice of 1 lime
1¼ pounds large shrimp, peeled and deveined
2 pounds small red bliss potatoes, halved
¼ cup vegetable oil
2 tablespoons plus 1 teaspoon curry powder
½ teaspoon kosher salt, plus more to taste
Black pepper, to taste
½ bunch kale, leaves stripped from the stem and torn into small pieces
1 cup panko breadcrumbs
½ cup sweetened shredded coconut
6 tablespoons salted butter, melted

1 Whisk the coconut milk, honey and lime juice in a large bowl. Add the shrimp and toss to coat. Cover and let marinate in the refrigerator, 15 to 20 minutes.

2 Meanwhile, position racks in the upper and lower thirds of the oven; preheat to 425°. Toss the potatoes with 2 tablespoons vegetable oil, 1 teaspoon curry powder, the salt and a few grinds of pepper in a bowl. Spread out on a rimmed baking sheet. Roast on the lower oven rack, turning, until browned, 20 minutes.

3 Toss the kale with the remaining 2 tablespoons vegetable oil in a medium bowl. Remove the baking sheet from the oven and toss the kale with the potatoes. Return to the oven and bake until the kale is crisp, 12 to 15 minutes; season with salt and pepper.

4 Meanwhile, combine the breadcrumbs, coconut and the remaining 2 tablespoons curry powder in a medium bowl. Stir in the melted butter until evenly combined.

5 Set a rack on another rimmed baking sheet. Pat the shrimp dry, then dredge in the breadcrumb mixture and place on the rack. Bake on the upper oven rack until the shrimp begin to curl and the breading is browned and crisp, 12 to 15 minutes. Serve the shrimp with the potatoes and kale.

STEP BY STEP

"*Everything in this dish is crispy: the shrimp, the potatoes and the kale!*"

"*Zucchini noodles are great for low-carb dinners!*"

Spicy Shrimp Stir-Fry with Zucchini Noodles

Prep time: 35 min ★ Total time: 45 min ★ Serves: 4 to 6

2 pounds zucchini noodles
½ cup low-sodium soy sauce
2 tablespoons oyster sauce
2 tablespoons sherry or dry white wine
1 tablespoon sugar
¼ teaspoon red pepper flakes
3 tablespoons peanut
   or vegetable oil

1 bunch scallions, whites thinly sliced, greens cut into 2-inch pieces
1½ pounds large shrimp, peeled and deveined
Kosher salt and black pepper, to taste
8 ounces baby bell peppers, thinly sliced into rings
1 small jalapeño pepper, thinly sliced
2 garlic cloves, minced
1 tablespoon minced fresh ginger

1 Bring a few cups of water to a boil in a large pot with a steamer basket in place. Add the zucchini noodles to the steamer, cover and cook, stirring halfway through, until tender, about 3 minutes. Remove the steamer basket to the sink and let the noodles drain and dry out a little.

2 Whisk the soy sauce, oyster sauce, sherry, sugar and red pepper flakes in a medium bowl. Set aside.

3 Heat 1 tablespoon peanut oil in a large skillet over high heat. Add the scallion greens and stir until charred, 30 to 45 seconds. Remove to a plate.

4 Pat the shrimp dry and season with salt and pepper. Add 1 tablespoon peanut oil to the skillet. Add half the shrimp in a single layer and cook, turning once, until opaque and cooked through, 3 to 4 minutes. Remove to the plate with the scallions. Repeat with the remaining shrimp; remove to the plate.

5 Let the pan get very hot again. Add the remaining 1 tablespoon peanut oil. Add the bell peppers and jalapeño and cook, stirring, until browned, 2 minutes. Reduce the heat to medium low and stir in the garlic, ginger and scallion whites; cook 1 to 2 more minutes.

6 Add the sauce to the skillet and heat through. Remove from the heat and toss in the shrimp and scallion greens. Serve over the zucchini noodles.

STEP BY STEP

Blackened Salmon with Edamame Succotash

Prep time: 30 min ★ Total time: 30 min ★ Serves: 4 to 6

2   teaspoons paprika
½   teaspoon dried oregano
¼   teaspoon cayenne pepper
1½   teaspoons garlic powder
1½   teaspoons onion powder
2   teaspoons kosher salt
Black pepper, to taste
1   large skin-on salmon fillet, about 2 pounds
4   tablespoons salted butter
1   onion, chopped
1   large red bell pepper, chopped
2   cups frozen shelled edamame
2   cups frozen corn
3   tablespoons red wine vinegar
¼   cup chopped fresh chives

1 Preheat the oven to 400°. Combine the paprika, oregano, cayenne, 1 teaspoon each garlic powder and onion powder, 1 teaspoon salt and a few grinds of pepper in a small bowl.

2 Line a rimmed baking sheet with foil. Place the salmon skin-side down on the pan and sprinkle with the spice mixture, pressing gently to adhere. Bake until the salmon is beginning to turn opaque and is just cooked through, 15 to 18 minutes.

3 Meanwhile, melt the butter in a large skillet over medium-high heat. Add the onion, bell pepper and the remaining 1 teaspoon salt and cook, stirring occasionally, until the vegetables are softened, 4 to 5 minutes.

4 Add the edamame to the skillet and cook, stirring, until warmed through, 2 to 3 minutes. Add the corn and the remaining ½ teaspoon each garlic powder and onion powder and cook, stirring occasionally, until the edamame is tender, 4 to 5 minutes. Stir in the vinegar and cook until absorbed, 1 to 2 minutes. Remove from the heat and stir in the chives. Slice the salmon and serve with the succotash.

STEP BY STEP

"I didn't start liking salmon until my 40s, so I'm making up for lost time!"

"*Fun fact: Caesar salad is one of my favorite room-service orders!*"

Chipotle Caesar Salad with Grilled Salmon

Prep time: 30 min ★ Total time: 30 min ★ Serves: 6

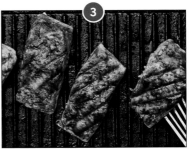

1	9-ounce loaf ciabatta bread, cut into 1-inch cubes
½	cup plus 1 tablespoon olive oil
1½	teaspoons kosher salt
	Black pepper, to taste
½	cup plus 2 tablespoons grated parmesan cheese
½	cup mayonnaise
¼	cup buttermilk
¼	cup sour cream
¼	cup plus 2 tablespoons adobo sauce (from a can of chipotles)
1	tablespoon balsamic vinegar
1	teaspoon Worcestershire sauce
1	anchovy fillet
1	garlic clove, smashed
6	6-ounce skin-on salmon fillets
1	head green-leaf lettuce, chopped
1	heart romaine lettuce, chopped

1. Preheat the oven to 400˚. For the croutons: Place the bread cubes on a baking sheet and toss with ½ cup olive oil, ½ teaspoon salt and a few grinds of pepper. Sprinkle with ½ cup of the parmesan and toss to coat. Bake until crisp and golden brown, 12 to 15 minutes. Set aside to cool.

2. Meanwhile, for the dressing: Combine the mayonnaise, buttermilk, sour cream, 2 tablespoons adobo sauce, the balsamic vinegar, Worcestershire sauce, anchovy, garlic, remaining 2 tablespoons parmesan, ¼ teaspoon salt and a few grinds of pepper in a blender and blend until smooth.

3. Preheat a grill or grill pan to medium. Brush the salmon with the remaining 1 tablespoon olive oil and season with ½ teaspoon salt and a few grinds of pepper. Grill skin-side up until marked and the salmon releases easily from the grill, 3 to 4 minutes. Flip and brush with the remaining ¼ cup adobo sauce. Continue to cook until the salmon is firm and cooked through, 10 to 12 minutes.

4. Combine both lettuces in a large bowl. Season with the remaining ¼ teaspoon salt and a few grinds of pepper. Add the dressing and toss to coat. Gently stir in the croutons. Serve the salmon on top of the salad.

Parmesan Fish Sticks
with Glazed Carrots

Prep time: 40 min ★ Total time: 50 min ★ Serves: 4 to 6

FISH STICKS

2	tablespoons olive oil
½	cup all-purpose flour
1	teaspoon kosher salt
½	teaspoon black pepper
1½	cups breadcrumbs
½	cup fresh parsley, chopped
3	tablespoons salted butter, melted
½	cup grated parmesan cheese
3	large eggs
2	pounds cod or haddock fillets

CARROTS

1½	pounds carrots, cut in half crosswise
2	tablespoons salted butter
2	tablespoons packed light brown sugar
½	teaspoon kosher salt
1	tablespoon apple cider vinegar
2	tablespoons fresh dill, finely chopped

1 For the fish: Preheat the oven to 450°. Brush a large rimmed baking sheet with the olive oil. Combine the flour, salt and pepper in a shallow bowl. Combine the breadcrumbs, parsley and melted butter in a separate shallow bowl and mix with a fork, then stir in the parmesan. Whisk the eggs in a third bowl.

2 Cut the fish into 1-inch-wide strips. Bread the fish by giving the strips a good coating of the seasoned flour, shaking off any excess. Dip in the beaten eggs until coated, then roll in the breadcrumb mixture, pressing to coat. Place the fish strips in a single layer on the baking sheet.

3 Bake the fish for 10 minutes, then flip and continue baking until the breading is golden and the fish is cooked through, another 5 to 8 minutes.

4 Meanwhile, for the carrots: Combine the carrots, butter, brown sugar, salt and ½ cup water in a large deep skillet over medium-high heat. Bring to a simmer, then cover and cook over medium heat until the carrots start softening, 4 to 6 minutes.

5 Uncover and cook until the water evaporates and the carrots are tender and glazed, 5 to 7 minutes more, adding the vinegar during the last minute of cooking. Remove from the heat, add the dill and toss. Serve with the fish sticks.

"*Fish sticks will forever remind me of my childhood. These are a grown-up version!*"

"This creamy avocado-lime mayo is what dreams are made of."

Blackened Salmon Burgers with Avocado-Lime Mayo

Prep time: 40 min ★ Total time: 40 min ★ Serves: 6

AVOCADO-LIME MAYO
⅓   cup mayonnaise
½   teaspoon kosher salt, plus more to taste
Grated zest and juice of 1 large lime
1   large avocado

SALMON BURGERS
1   tablespoon kosher salt
4   teaspoons sweet paprika
2   teaspoons garlic powder
2   teaspoons onion powder
1   teaspoon dried oregano
1   teaspoon black pepper
½   teaspoon cayenne pepper
Cooking spray
2   pounds skinless salmon fillets, cut into 1-inch chunks
3   tablespoons mayonnaise
½   cup panko breadcrumbs
4   scallions, sliced
¼   cup vegetable oil
6   potato hamburger buns, split
Sliced tomatoes, sliced red onion and lettuce leaves, for topping
Potato chips, for serving

1. For the avocado-lime mayo: Puree the mayonnaise, salt, lime zest and juice and the avocado in a food processor until smooth. Season with more salt, if needed. Scrape into a bowl and press plastic wrap on the surface; refrigerate until ready to serve. Wipe out the food processor.
2. For the burgers: Mix the salt, paprika, garlic and onion powders, oregano, black pepper and cayenne in a bowl.
3. Preheat the oven to 350°. Line a baking sheet with parchment paper and spray with cooking spray. Pulse half of the salmon in the food processor until chopped into small pieces. Transfer to a large bowl. Add the remaining salmon to the processor along with the mayonnaise; blend until mostly smooth. Add to the chopped salmon, along with the panko, scallions and half of the spice mix. Mix well.
4. Form the salmon mixture into six 4-inch patties on the baking sheet. Season both sides with the remaining spice mix. Put the buns cut-side up on a second baking sheet. Bake until toasted, 5 minutes.
5. Heat 2 tablespoons oil in a large cast-iron skillet over medium-high heat. Add 3 patties and cook until browned, 3 to 4 minutes per side. Wipe out the skillet; repeat with the remaining oil and patties. Serve on the buns with the avocado-lime mayo, tomatoes, onion and lettuce. Serve with chips.

STEP BY STEP

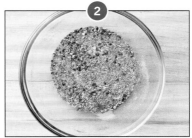

Grilled Shrimp Flatbreads

Prep time: 30 min ★ Total time: 30 min ★ Serves: 6

2	cups packed fresh cilantro
2	cups packed fresh parsley
¼	cup packed fresh mint
4	garlic cloves, grated
2	tablespoons red wine vinegar
1	teaspoon red pepper flakes
½	teaspoon kosher salt

	Black pepper, to taste
¾	cup olive oil, plus more for the grill
2	pounds medium shrimp, peeled and deveined
⅔	cup mayonnaise
6	pieces naan
½	small red onion, thinly sliced
2	plum tomatoes, chopped

1 For the herb sauce: Combine the cilantro, parsley, mint and 2 cloves garlic in a blender or food processor. Add the vinegar, red pepper flakes, ½ teaspoon salt and a few grinds of pepper and pulse a few times. Slowly pour in the olive oil, pulsing, until mostly smooth.

2 Transfer the sauce to a large bowl, reserving ½ cup for topping. Add the shrimp to the large bowl and toss to coat completely.

3 Mix the mayonnaise and remaining 2 cloves garlic in a small bowl and set aside.

4 Preheat a grill pan or grill to medium high. Lightly oil the pan or grates. Grill the naan, a few pieces at a time, until marked, 1 to 2 minutes per side. Stack on a platter and cover with a towel to keep warm.

5 Add half of the shrimp to the grill in a single layer (use a grill basket if using an outdoor grill) and cook until lightly charred and beginning to turn pink, 1 to 2 minutes per side. Remove to a plate and repeat with the remaining shrimp.

6 Spread the naan with the garlic mayonnaise. Top with the shrimp, red onion and tomatoes and drizzle with the reserved herb sauce.

STEP BY STEP

"This herb sauce is so fresh and fragrant. I like drizzling it on steak, too!"

"I'm obsessed with everything about this spicy-sweet sauce."

Sweet Chili Shrimp Sauté

Prep time: 30 min ★ Total time: 30 min ★ Serves: 4 to 6

2½	teaspoons kosher salt
1	cup white rice
½	cup Thai sweet chili sauce
2	tablespoons rice vinegar
2	tablespoons soy sauce
2	teaspoons Sriracha
2	teaspoons cornstarch
5	tablespoons vegetable oil
1½	pounds peeled and deveined large shrimp
2	large carrots, thinly sliced into half-moons
1	medium red onion, sliced
½	medium head green cabbage, roughly chopped
4	ounces snow peas, trimmed and halved crosswise
½	cup salted peanuts (optional)

1 Combine 2 cups water and 1 teaspoon salt in a medium saucepan and bring to a boil. Stir in the rice and reduce to a simmer, then cover and cook until the rice is tender, 18 to 20 minutes. Remove from the heat and let sit, covered, for 5 minutes. Fluff with a fork.

2 Meanwhile, in a small bowl, stir together the chili sauce, vinegar, soy sauce and Sriracha. Stir in the cornstarch until completely smooth.

3 Heat 2 tablespoons vegetable oil in a large skillet over high heat. Season the shrimp with 1 teaspoon salt, then add to the skillet and cook, tossing occasionally, until just cooked through, 3 to 4 minutes. Remove to a plate.

4 Add the remaining 3 tablespoons oil to the skillet over high heat. Add the carrots, red onion and cabbage. Season with the remaining ½ teaspoon salt and cook, tossing, until the vegetables are crisp-tender and beginning to brown around the edges, about 4 minutes. Add the snow peas along with the shrimp and toss to combine.

5 Add the chili sauce mixture, toss and bring to a simmer. Cook, tossing to coat everything in the sauce, about 1 minute. Serve with the rice and sprinkle with the peanuts.

STEP BY STEP

Notes

The Pioneer Woman is a registered trademark of The Pioneer Woman, LLC

Photographs by Ghazalle Badiozamani: 32, 101, 158;
Danielle Daly: 36, 39, 40, 43, 70, 73, 74, 109, 142, 145, 146, 165, 166;
Ryan Dausch: 15, 16, 19, 20, 23, 24, 27, 28, 49, 50, 53, 54, 57, 58, 61, 85, 86, 89, 90, 117, 118, 121, 122, 125, 126, 133, 150, 153, 154, 157;
Ryan Liebe: 15, 49, 50, 117, 150; Con Poulos: 11, 12, 82, 114;
Ralph Smith: 31, 35, 44, 62, 65, 66, 69, 77, 78, 93, 94, 97, 98, 102, 105, 106, 110, 129, 130, 134, 137, 138, 141, 161, 162, 169

Book design by Lauren Vitello

Recipes from *The Pioneer Woman Magazine*

Library of Congress Cataloging-in-Publication Data is on file with the publisher.

ISBN 978-1-955710-11-4

Printed in China

2 4 6 8 10 9 7 5 3 paperback

HEARST